ESCAPING THE DRIFT

ESCAPING THE DRIFT

HOW TO MAKE THE WORLD HAPPEN **FOR** YOU, NOT **TO** YOU

JOHN GAFFORD

RADIUS BOOK GROUP
NEW YORK

Radius Book Group
A division of Diversion Publishing Corp.
www.radiusbookgroup.com

For more information, email info@radiusbookgroup.com
First Edition: November 2025

Hardcover ISBN: 979-8-89515-077-1
e-ISBN: 979-8-89515-114-3

Design by Neuwirth & Associates, Inc.
Cover design by Will Mack

Printed in the United States of America
1 3 5 7 9 10 8 6 4 2

In loving memory
of my dear friend Steve Sims.

CONTENTS

CONTENTS

FOREWORD

I don't write forewords often. In fact, I don't write them unless I'm genuinely moved—unless someone's work has such an impact that I can't ignore it. So I'm not doing this lightly. *Escaping the Drift* by John Gafford isn't just another book—it's a wake-up call wrapped in a challenge. John isn't here to give you fluffy words or empty motivation. He's here to rip through the nonsense and show you the cold, hard truth about how to stop drifting through life.

John grabs you by the collar, shakes off all the excuses you've been hiding behind, and pushes you into the uncomfortable truth that life is happening right now—and if you don't take control, it'll pass you by. This isn't the book for the passive reader. This is for the person ready to get out of neutral and make things happen. If you've been coasting through life, this book will rip the autopilot right out of you and slap you back into the driver's seat.

If you're ready for a punch in the gut that will wake you up, then this book is exactly what you need. Don't expect any sugarcoating or "easy road" BS. This is the straight talk, the real stuff, and John delivers it in a way that will get under your skin and force you to think differently about how you show up in the world.

I'm telling you, read this book. But don't read it if you're not ready to take action, because once you do, there's no going back.

—STEVE SIMS,
author of *Bluefishing* & *Go for Stupid*

PREFACE

Have you ever walked into a bank, scared to apply for a checking account because your credit was so bad you could only hope you wouldn't be declined? Have you ever lost sleep, wondering if tonight was the night the repo man was going to show up and take your car even though you parked it around the corner? Have you ever been so completely at the mercy of your job that your whole identity got destroyed in an instant when you got the notice you were no longer needed?

I have.

At twenty-seven years old, I was drifting. Not in control, not charting my own course—just floating along wherever life decided to take me. I wasn't broke, but I wasn't successful. I wasn't happy, but I wasn't miserable. I was just . . . existing.

And let me tell you, nothing in life is more dangerous than existing without direction.

When you drift, you become a victim of circumstance. You don't make choices; they get made for you. You don't create opportunities; you wait and hope they show up. You live reactively, not proactively. And worst of all, you tell yourself that this is just how life is. That this is what being an adult looks like. That people like you don't get to live extraordinary lives.

That's all bullshit.

I wrote this book as a user's manual to my twenty-seven-year-old self. If I could go back in time and hand myself a guide on how to stop drifting and start thriving, this would be it. The concepts in this book aren't complicated. There's no secret formula, no magic bullet. But what I can promise you is that if you're willing to put in the work—if you're ready to take responsibility for your life instead of letting the current carry you wherever it wants—you can transform your reality in ways you never thought possible.

I know this because I did it.

I went from worrying about making my next car payment to building multiple seven-figure businesses. I went from feeling stuck in an ordinary life to creating a life on my terms, doing what I want, when I want. And I didn't do it because I was smarter, luckier, or had some kind of advantage you don't. I did it because I stopped drifting. I took control.

That's what this book is about.

This isn't some abstract, feel-good self-help book that just tells you to "believe in yourself" and leaves it at that. This is a road map. A system. A framework you can use to identify what's holding you back, break free from it, and start building the life you actually want.

No situation is permanent—unless you choose to stay in it.

If you're reading this, you already know that something has to change. Maybe you don't know exactly what's wrong, but you know you're capable of more. You know there's another level of life that other people seem to have figured out, and you're tired of watching from the sidelines.

Good.

That means you're ready.

It's time to Break Free. Level Up. Live on Purpose.

Let's get to work.

INTRODUCTION

SWIMMING WITH SHARKS

HOW DISHONESTY CAN LEAD TO THE DRIFT

Let's talk about *The Apprentice*. Everybody asks.

I was one of the eighteen candidates on Season 3 of the show, and—spoiler alert—I got fired. But half a season on the air was plenty of time to gather up lessons in business, in life, and, of course, in reality television.

For instance, do you know what a "dummy cast" is? I sure didn't.

Back in 2005, before there were dozens and dozens of reality shows on dozens and dozens of networks, *The Apprentice* was a big deal. So big, in fact, that multitudes of fans used to follow the production around New York City to see who was in the cast and what kind of trouble they were getting into. The producers were intent on keeping the candidates and the tasks secret, which meant a whole lot of sneaking around. And it wasn't easy, because you can't really hide on the streets of New York City.

Regular *Apprentice* viewers will recall that when one of the show's candidates was fired, you'd see them walking out of Trump Tower and getting into a cab, after which they'd head off to points unknown. The cab shots weren't filmed right after host Donald Trump said, "You're fired," but rather on a random day at three in the morning. In order to work that subterfuge, the set would be populated with not just the cast, but also two hundred actors, aka, the dummy cast.

The TV crew would walk us out of the building, one by one, cast and dummy cast alike, where we'd march into a taxi, the camera following us the whole way. That's two hundred–plus different cab shots, all so the fans and the paparazzi had no way of knowing who was really on the show. (Yes, there were fans and paparazzi watching us in the middle of the night. Even in its Season 3 infancy, that show was a massive deal.) Additionally, when we were running around New York doing our tasks, there were teams of actors and camera crews running around in other areas of the city, doing similar stuff as us, hopefully throwing off anyone who could possibly ruin any surprises for the viewers.

When you're in the midst of all this madness, the last thing you'd expect is to have a life-changing epiphany. This is why you always pay attention to the world around you, even when the world around you is filled with nervous production assistants, nosy journalists, and the threat of getting fired on national television.

One particularly dreary New York October day, about a month into shooting, we were in front of Trump Tower, prepping for our next task. It was one of those days where you could just tell *everything* was going wrong with production. There were technical problems, there were logistical problems, and the vibe wasn't great.

Enter the show's creator and producer, Mark Burnett.

Before filming started, I studied up on the British television magnate's background because I wanted to know who I'd be working for—and that's the same way I'd approach *any* meeting to this day, whether it's with one of the most infamous TV producers in the world or . . . you. When it comes to business, it behooves *everybody* to prepare for *everything*.

I learned that Mark began his professional life in America as a Beverly Hills nanny, soon after which the patriarch of the family for whom he was nannying hired him to work at his insurance company, after which Mark decided to set up a T-shirt shop on Venice Beach. From there, it was television, international acclaim, and a hefty bank account. The guy had it figured out.

On the morning in question, the crew was running around like their hair was on fire—you could almost see the thought bubbles saying, *Oh shit, this is going south and Mark's gonna be pissed*—and there's Mark, sure enough, looking and acting pissed, and understandably so. I don't think he was being a prick on purpose, per se. Mark's leadership style, from my perspective at the time, was extremely intense and high-pressure—not surprising given the stakes involved.

When he stomped by me, I was standing next to another candidate, a real estate financier named Kristen Kirchner. Kristen was a good person, but she could be brusque—although I think that was the idea. The producers cast type A, alpha personalities who wouldn't always get along. After all, friendship on a reality show can make for crappy television.

In what I assume was an attempt to lighten his mood, Kristen called out to him, "Treading water today, Mark?"

Mark stopped in his tracks. He gave Kristen a death stare and growled, "I never tread water. I swim." And then he stomped off.

I looked around at my fellow cast members. We were all silent, but I could tell by the expression on everybody's face that they were thinking basically the same thing I was: *Oh my God, don't mess with Mark*.

But . . . I *never tread water. I swim.* Damn. That's one hell of a line.

For Mark Burnett, this was a tiny moment in a life filled with gigantic moments. Likely in his mind, we were all spokes in his wheel, gears in his mechanism, and when a part of his machine malfunctioned, he didn't ruminate on it—he figured out how to fix it. That hit me on a gut level because Mark was the guy who created not only *The Apprentice*, but also the *Survivor* franchise. I was a guy who'd worked at Hooters.

For me, the biggest takeaway from that moment was, no matter what's going on, no matter which camera is malfunctioning, no matter which cast member is having a meltdown, Mark Burnett was going to push through it and remain (relatively) unfazed. How can you not respect that? How can you not take it to heart? This is a guy who went from being a nanny to one of the globe's most successful entertainment moguls. When he discusses how he got to where he got—and, more importantly, how he stayed there—you pay attention.

It was an aha moment for me, and I'll give myself credit because I recognized right then and there that it was an aha moment. (Sometimes you don't realize you heard or saw something important and meaningful until hours, or days, or weeks, or months later.) After Mark dropped that line, I thought, *That dude came up with something that's really resonating with me. That's some gangster shit.* The funny thing was it's possible Mark said that simply as a way to shut Kristen up, but wisdom can come from the oddest places.

In that second, I saw how you can fall into one or two categories: You're either somebody **who the world is happening to**, or you're somebody **who's happening to the world**. Regardless of how swift the stream is coming at you, or how high the fires are burning, it's up to you to charge forward. To that point, I was often one of those guys who, when faced with adversity, would throw his hands in the air, say, "Well, this is totally screwed," and pivot away from it, instead of figuring out how to improve and grow. I was treading, not swimming.

I was stuck in The Drift. And I was far from the only Drifter the world had seen.

Look at Robert Downey Jr. He had some early success (*Less Than Zero*, *The Pick-Up Artist*), then early-mid career Drifting (falling asleep in strangers' backyards after a three-day coke binge), then he became Tony Stark.

Look at Grant Cardone. He went from Drifting as a car salesman, to Drifting as a substance addict, to not Drifting as a bajillionaire real estate mogul.

The Drift is when you find yourself letting life happen to you rather than proactively impacting your life.

The Drift is when you find yourself going sideways, from job to job, from relationship to relationship, from flatline to flatline.

The Drift is when you find yourself treading water while keeping your head just above the surface.

The Drift is when you find yourself Drifting and you don't even realize it.

Prior to *The Apprentice*, I was in full Drift mode, always waiting for somebody to save me, be it a girlfriend, or an employer, or my father. My future success always seemed to be in the control of others . . . or at least that's how it felt. The whole thing reminds me of the moment from the best Christmas movie ever, *Die Hard* (yes, it *is* a Christmas movie!), when one of the evil henchmen tells John McClane, "Why don't you come out? I won't hurt you. No one's coming to help you."

I should've taken that to heart, right?

Sure, I had some cool jobs and did some fun stuff, but I never made any real money, never had anything I could say was a true success. At the time, if you would've asked me how things were going in both my personal and professional life, I probably would've said, "It's all great!" But the truth was, I didn't have anything *substantial* going on, anything that satisfied my soul, anything that might lead me toward a fruitful future, anything that made my bank account happy. My experiences on *The Apprentice* were key in transitioning my thought process, in teaching me what success is, and how to make *it* happen.

I didn't realize how much I was Drifting until I saw somebody who was swimming, and swimming.

Break Free. Level Up. Live on Purpose.

Before we go any further, let's get real. Answer these questions honestly—no sugarcoating, no excuses.

1. Do you feel like most days are just "on repeat" without real progress toward something bigger?
2. Are you waiting for the "right time" to make a change, but that time never seems to come?
3. Do you let external circumstances—your boss, your finances, your family, the economy—dictate your choices?
4. Are you more reactive than proactive, constantly putting out fires instead of building something meaningful?
5. Do you spend more time scrolling through social media, binge-watching shows, or numbing out than you do actively improving your situation?
6. When you think about your future, do you feel excitement, or just uncertainty and anxiety?
7. Do you have clear, written goals for your life, or are you just hoping things "work out"?

8. Are you surrounded by people who challenge you to be better, or are you just going along with the crowd?

9. Have you been in the same financial, career, or personal situation for years with little to no progress?

10. Do you secretly feel like you were meant for more, but don't know how to make it happen?

If you answered "yes" to more than a couple of these, chances are you're in The Drift. And once you're aware, you have a choice: Stay where you are, or start taking control.

The rest of this book is going to show you exactly how to escape The Drift and take charge of your life. But no one can do the work for you. You have to make the decision: Will you keep floating, or will you start swimming toward the life you actually want?

Your move.

ESCAPING THE DRIFT

CHAPTER 1

HONESTY WITH YOURSELF

BURNING DOWN THE HOUSE

Honesty is innate. Dishonesty is learned. We're not hardwired to be untruthful with others or with ourselves. We acquire that unfortunate mindset as a defense mechanism. That's something I learned the hard way.

My family lived in a tiny town in North Florida, so far north you could call it Baja, Georgia. When I was young, we moved into a country club in the ritziest neighborhood of town, right on the golf course, soon after which my parents got divorced. My dad, who was an attorney, really buried my mother in the split, so there we were, living in the ritziest neighborhood, but we didn't have any money, and it was hard to make ends meet. While my dad did make sure we didn't starve, we weren't living the lives of our next-door neighbors. It created this weird family dynamic where I overcompensated for our lack of *things* by lying about all kinds of nonsense. And oftentimes, my little white lies would turn into gigantic whoppers.

Like the fire.

When I was about twelve years old, my friend Corey and I were at my house playing "match flip." What's match flip, you might ask? Well, match flip is when you take a big wooden kitchen match, light it, and flip it. Super responsible game for a twelve-year-old, right? Compounding the lack of responsibility was the fact that we were playing this *inside the house.*

One Saturday morning, in the midst of a particularly good match flip session, there was a knock at the front door, a big wooden door with a messed-up lock that made it difficult to open. After I finally cracked the thing, two of my sister Mandy's friends—who, truth be told, were kind of juvenile delinquent dudes—asked to borrow a hose for the school's car wash. Suddenly, I felt a smack on my shoulder. I turned around. It was Corey. He had a horrified look on his face.

Our drapes were on fire.

I froze. Now before you cast aspersions upon my inability to act quickly and decisively, remember that I was twelve.

To their credit, those two juvenile delinquents ran around the back of the house and, before the fire got too out of control, found our garden hose and put it out... but not before the couch, the carpet, the drapes, and the ceiling all suffered severe fire damage.

I said to Corey, "My mother's going to kill me. She's literally going to kill me."

One of the JDs seemingly took pity on me and said, "You guys take off and come back in two hours and act like you don't know what's going on. We're gonna get you out of this."

I said, "All right, fine," then left. Not a fantastic idea, but again, I was twelve.

After two hours of walking around the neighborhood, Corey and I made it back to the house. My mother was standing on the lawn, aghast. There were four police cars on the street, lights flashing.

I sidled up to my mom and, with complete wide-eyed innocence, asked, "What's going on?"

My mother silently pointed into the house, and I completely understood why she couldn't speak. Aside from the fact that much of the living room was burnt to a crisp, those two JDs had taken our crappy 1979 TV and our worthless stereo and set it outside in the backyard.

Apparently the JDs told the cops that when they came to get the hose, they saw two guys break into the house. They painted themselves as the heroes, saying that the imaginary burglars tried to burn the house down as the JDs chased them out, after which they put out the fire.

As I listened to that pile of crap, I thought, *No way are they buying this.* I couldn't speak.

The police officer—who was part of a force that nobody would consider one of the better law enforcement organizations in the state—nodded and said, "Yeah, this is what they do. They break in and try to steal stuff and burn the place down to cover their tracks." And that was the end of it. To my astonishment, the insurance company covered the damage. I kept quiet about what really happened for years—immature and terrified of the consequences.

The problem was, since I did get away scot-free, lying became a pattern. Once you fall into that pattern, it's hard to get out. Consistent dishonesty leads directly to The Drift. If you're false with yourself and with others, there's no way you'll be anything but stuck. How can you improve your lot in life if you're always trying to keep track of your lies?

Did the fire teach me a lasting lesson? Nah.

Fast-forward five years. My mother had moved to Tallahassee, and I was spending the summer with my father. One night, a few friends and I met some high school girls. We snuck them out of their respective houses and brought them back to my dad's, where we hung out until the wee hours—let's call it four in the morning. Like the responsible gentlemen we were, we took the girls home. After dropping them off at their subdivision, I turned onto the main street, where a truck came out of nowhere and swerved us off the road.

Out of the truck jumped two large, angry redneck fathers. One of them roared, "Did you just drop two girls off back there?"

I said, "Yes."

Simultaneously, one of my buddies said, "No."

The rednecks silently glared at us for a few seconds, after which the angrier one said, "Follow us back to the house."

This is what I said to my friends: "Oh shit. Oh shit. Oh shit. Oh shit." Which summed it up pretty nicely.

Here's the thing: Burning down the house notwithstanding, I was basically a good kid who hung out with other basically good kids. I was smart, I earned decent grades, and I rarely caused any problems at school. Potential violence was all new to me, so my freak-out was understandable.

When we arrived back at the subdivision, we were met by a bunch of angry fathers standing on the lawn. It was a sea of dirty baseball caps, ZZ Top beards, old Levi jeans, overhanging beer bellies, and pissed-off facial expressions. One of the beard-o's stepped forward and, *bam*, kicked and broke one of my headlights.

I said, "Oh, we're dead meat. Stay in the car, stay in the car, stay in the car."

My friend Jesse said, "Nope. I'm getting out."

As Jesse opened the door, one of the rednecks yelled, "Stay in the car!"

Jesse didn't stay in the car.

I said, "Oh my God, what are you doing?"

The redneck screamed, "I told you to stay in the car! You want me to kick your ass?"

Jesse pointed at me and said, "His dad's an attorney. You touch me, I'll sue you for everything you have."

Thanks, Jesse. I told him, "Get in the car. Get in the car."

Right then, thank God, a deputy sheriff rolled up. After surveying the scene he told me to open my window, then said, "I should take you to jail for contributing to the delinquency of minors."

I said, "Well, wait a second, dude—we're minors. How am I contributing to the delinquency of a minor when I'm a minor? I'm not eighteen. I'm not an adult."

The deputy didn't like that. In retrospect, I can't blame him.

Glaring at me, he said, "Okay, I'm going to see your dad tomorrow at the courthouse and I'm going to tell him all about this. Get out of here."

So we got out of there without sustaining any further headlight damage.

When I got home, without even considering the consequences, I woke up my dad and told him the complete truth. He grounded me—as well he should have, in part because I shouldn't have put myself in that situation in the first place, and in part because I was already grounded.

Oops.

You see, I was busted with a cooler full of empty beer cans in the parking lot of my high school during our last day before summer vacation. When I got caught, I was suspended for the beginning of the next school year... but I didn't care because I knew I was moving to Tallahassee with my mother. That all being the case, I jumped on the grenade and protected my buddies.

I assumed the deputy would tell my father what happened, and, due to double jeopardy, I would've gotten into worse trouble. In other words, I preemptively told him because I assumed the deputy would anyway, and I was trying to avoid getting into further trouble for keeping it quiet. Thing is, *the deputy never informed my father*. Effectively, I told on myself, and the moral of that particular story is, **forced truth is not real truth**. Had I not been previously grounded, I likely would've kept my mouth shut.

If you're coerced to tell the truth about a given situation—whether it's dropping a truth bomb on either somebody else or yourself—you might not tell the complete truth, and then you've boxed yourself in with your half-truth. You're circumventing fate. It's better just to be entirely truthful in the first place. Ya keep lying, ya keep Drifting.

This applies to business, as well. Two hours before I sat down to write this, I was on a call discussing private money, and bringing investors into deals. I pointed out to my colleague that one of the things you *have* to do when you work with investors on a deal—*any* type of deal—is give them a steady flow of feedback and a steady flow of information, whether the feedback or information is good or bad.

My colleague asked, "What if you do a private money deal and the deal goes bad and the people lose their money?"

I said, "They should have known for six months there was a possibility they could lose their money, not just the day the deal closes. If you wait until the end, it doesn't work; you lose the trust of a potential partner, and you look terrible."

By giving people a steady stream of information that allows your associates, your friends, or your family to see the situation for what it is and not just the end result, you will avoid that. Too often, when things start to go south, we conceal things from others... and we conceal things from ourselves. We try to paint pictures rosier than they are, and then when things get completely screwed, you're completely screwed.

I'm a real estate guy, so here's a real estate analogy: Consistent dishonesty ruins any kind of foundation you might build.

If you build a house on a foundation that was poured incorrectly or poorly, your project is done before it even gets going. For example, a few weeks back, I started having issues with a house that we built—specifically, the drains upstairs were flowing slowly. It was going to be incredibly expensive for me to fix the house because the pipes weren't done right from the top to the bottom all the way into the foundation; we were going to have to rip everything out and start from scratch, which was going to be a pain in the ass. Could it have been avoided? Hell yes, but it needed to have been caught early. Once the foundation was laid over the top of the plumbing, the problem was buried... temporarily.

Burying things in that manner—which, when you think about it, is another form of dishonesty—is one of the things that leads to The Drift. Think about it: In order to set yourself up for long-term success, you've got to be completely transparent with yourself. If you don't understand where you are or where you're going, you're screwed. When you begin a journey, you choose a destination and figure out the best way to get there... but if you're not honest about where you are, your compass is never going to work correctly.

I think everybody gets so focused on where they want to go that they don't take the time to focus on where they currently are. This may sound super-simple, but before you start your journey—be it personal or professional—get a blank piece of paper and write down where you are... and be 200 percent honest with yourself. Look at yourself in the metaphorical mirror, take in the warts and all, consider everything that's good, or bad, or ugly, and write it down. If you don't feel like you can be truthful, write it down. If you think you have a tendency to be lazy, write it down. If you're known to procrastinate, write it down. Because if you don't start with that foundation of truth and understanding, you can't build anything of quality on top of that. And if you do start building without laying the groundwork, you're going to have metaphorical and literal plumbing problems for years.

Even to this day, any time I'm going through adversity, I pull out the paper and get real with myself. For that matter, as I write this, I'm dealing with adversity galore. And I'm far from alone.

As I write this, the mortgage market has changed on us. The market *always* changes on us; it's just a matter of to what degree. So, considering the volatility of our economy, this advice isn't time sensitive. It's eternal. Unfortunately. Today, our real estate sales volume is down 45 percent, so we've had to make considerable cuts in all our businesses, we've had to ask people to take salary reductions, and we're even considering closing down a couple of joint venture partnerships.

These are difficult decisions, easily the most difficult of my job. In order to try and wrap my head around them, I'll pull out that blank sheet of paper and draw up a list: *Where am I? What have I done? What am I doing right now? Is my effort where it should be? Is this branch failing because of lack of ingenuity on our behalf, or is it just failing because it's failing? Is the market failing that branch or are we failing that branch?*

If the answer is that we're failing it, we need to acknowledge and accept that. We can't change the market, but we can change our approach and ask ourselves questions like:

What's the problem as I see it?

What do I think caused this?

What did I do to contribute to it?

What external forces helped cause it?

Who do I know that may have been through something similar, and can thus help me?

What's the worst-case scenario?

What's the best-case scenario?

What happens if I act right away?

What happens if I don't act right away?

Is there another way to accomplish my goal?

Along those lines, one of my favorite maxims is, *Stop pointing the finger and start pulling the thumb*, and that's a maxim I live by when things are good or bad. Back when I was Drifting, when I faced adversity, I'd moan, *Why is this happening to me?* rather than, *What have I done to cause this?*

Admittedly, sometimes you haven't messed up at all, but you should *always* look for the internal solution first, because you don't have any control over 99 percent of the world around you. You *do*, however, have 100 percent control over what you can personally do, or how you interpret information, or what kind of effort you can put forth. If you start with the one thing you can actually control, your results are generally going to be far better and considerably more efficient.

This kind of self-examination can take you out of your comfort zone, but that's not a bad thing, as comfort can kill your drive and lead you into a modified version of The Drift. You have to focus on proper effort, and to illustrate, let's go with a football metaphor.

Let's say that touchdowns were worth ten points and field goals were worth six, instead of seven and three. Would the scores of games that were, say, 27–20 still be 27–20? Nope, the scores would be much higher. The players and coaches don't care how many points they get for a touchdown. They care about executing the next play. They care about their individual effort. They care about not letting their teammates down. They care about holding on to the ball. They care about blocking. They don't care whether a trip to the end zone gets them seven or ten or one hundred points. If you were to raise the points in a football game, the scores would be exponentially higher, but the effort on the field would remain the same.

That attitude applies to real estate. Here in my current hometown of Las Vegas, back in 2014, the average sale price of a house was around $200,000. Now, ten years later, it's $500,000. By that math, you'd think Realtors would be making more than double as much money, because we get paid on a percentage of the price of the house as it's sold. Truth be told, most Realtors that were making $60,000 ten years ago are still making the inflationary equivalent of $60,000, because they're not focused on the effort they put forth every day; they're focused on the dollar figure they need to earn, because that's what creates comfort. Rather than focusing on the result of the dollar figure, they should focus on the effort they put forth every day. If they took that approach, their results, both sales-wise and income-wise, would grow exponentially.

All this stuff is intangible. You can't quantify honesty or foundation. But if you need a number, sometimes you have to reset to zero.

When I was stuck in The Drift, I would freak out when my bank account hit zero, but as long as I could scramble and cover my bills, I thought everything was fine. So my definition of broke then was actually BROKE. Today, if I have less than a six-figure number of accessible cash, I freak out. So that's now my zero; that's now my broke... which is why you have to change your zero.

I break everything down into what I call MOLs, or months of life, and it again involves being honest with yourself.

I figure anybody, with the proper effort and focus, can turn things around in twelve months. But a year can seem daunting, so you need to stack those months of life and let six months become your zero and build your financial cushion however you possibly can, whether it's finding a new job, or adding side hustles to your current gig. When you have your six MOLs settled—when you have a little bit of a cushion—you can start to take some risk and push forward in a different way. When you're always worried about getting back to zero, you get caught in this hamster wheel. But just like the negatives that can cause The Drift, too much comfort can as well. Once you hit the point of having a nice safety net, you need to forget you have it. Knowing you're safe can lead to complacency and straight to The Drift.

One good way to avoid complacency is to have multiple bank accounts.

In real estate, we tend to get our money in big chunks. If you get a big check and that check goes into an account, when you roll up to the ATM and see this large pile of money, it could psychologically screw up your chances to succeed, because you're going to think, *Oh man, I got plenty of bread. I can take the day off. I don't need to do work today because I can afford to buy this, and I have enough cash to travel there*. You need to have an account that's only for your bills, and the account balance should cover your bills, and little else. All your other money should go into an account that you can't mess with at the ATM, some sort of savings account that you have to deal with at the bank. DO NOT connect it to your other accounts online because going to the bank can suck, and if you have to deal with it at the bank, you'll be way less likely to touch it.

This may seem simplistic, but don't think you're above any of this, as ego can also hold you back…and I have one of those. I even did when I was dealing with The Drift. To paraphrase Marcellus Wallace in *Pulp Fiction*, "Fuck ego. Ego only hurts. It never helps."

When I wasn't succeeding, I still thought I was more important than I was, because I had some cool jobs, like running a club in Atlanta called Cobalt, a place that *Esquire* magazine called the number one nightclub on the East Coast. (*Much* more about Cobalt later.)

Once I was informed by my doctor that the nightlife business was actually killing me, I knew I needed a change. I was often told that I should be in sales, so I called my buddy Rick Wells, who was the vice president of the giant—and ultimately shady—telecommunications company WorldCom (Google it), and told him, "Give me a job selling telecom."

Rick was a good friend whom I figured would hook me up. He didn't, explaining, "Bro, I can't hire you off the street to sell telecom. You gotta go get some sales experience."

"Okay, what should I do?"

"You've got two choices: You can go sell Kirby vacuum cleaners, or you can go sell cars. Doing either will get you a PhD in sales in ninety days."

I said, "Well, there's no way I'm going to sell Kirby vacuum cleaners door-to-door—zero chance. And I really don't want to sell cars."

Rick said, "Go sell cars."

That would be a huge kick in the nuts, going from being a super-cool nightclub guy to a car salesman, but it was a means to an end, a way to get out of The Drift. I looked in the paper and, sure enough, there was an ad for a job fair at an auto dealership. I landed a gig at Troncalli Nissan in the Decatur section of Atlanta. My first month there, I sold thirty cars, which was almost like bowling a perfect game. And Rick was 100 percent right: I really did get a doctorate in sales.

If you've ever bought a car, you know the drill: You go to the dealership, you take a car out on a test-drive, then you sit down in a little cubicle with a salesman, where they'll say, "What do you want to pay?" After you give them your figure, they'll make a show of leaving the cubicle and walking over to the sales manager, then returning and saying, "This is what we can do."

When I first started, the sales manager would tell me, "The best we can do is...," and then he'd give me his number, and I'd believe him. After I was there for a while, I realized that I could do better on the final numbers because I'd seen *other* salespeople do better on the final numbers. So I started giving better final numbers, working faster, and cutting to the chase, which allowed me to move more units.

One of the most memorable lessons came from a used car manager named James Myrick. James was like Don King: brash, bold, lots of rings, and a gold tooth, the kind of straight shooter who'd tell a customer about his trade-in. "This car's been hit more times than Joe Louis. It's a piece of shit."

Late one morning, a potential customer was trying to lowball me, and their numbers were so crazy that I knew we wouldn't be able to make it work...but he wouldn't give up. He sat in my office, pounded on my desk, and said, "We're not leaving until we pay *this*!"

This went on for three hours.

By the time they gave up and left, it was about 3:00 PM, and I was exhausted and frustrated. James read the expression on my face and said, "Having a bad day, John?"

I said, "Yeah, that guy just wasted my entire morning and afternoon. It was ridiculous."

"Did you miss lunch?" he asked.

"Yeah."

"Come on, I'll get you something to eat."

"I'm not hungry."

"Come with me anyway."

I shrugged. "Fine."

We walked across the street to Blimpie. As we waited in line, he told me how great I was doing, then asked, "You sure you don't want anything?"

"I'm sure."

He said, "Suit yourself," then told the cashier, "I'll have a twelve-inch cold cut combo, and put this on it, and put that on it, and some more of this, and some more of that."

The cashier rang him up and said, "That'll be $7.99."

James said, "Oh no, I can get that same sub for $3 down the street. I'll give you $3.50 for it."

"No. No, no. $7.99."

"I'll give you $4.00."

"No, $7.99."

"All I've got is $4.00."

The cashier slammed the register shut and said, "Get out of my store!"

Once we were outside, James asked, "Do you feel better now?"

I said, "Not really. Maybe."

In his own twisted way, James Myrick—the Don King of used cars—was trying to show me that any sale can fall apart, any customer can be unreasonable, and you can't let a small experience like this send you Drifting.

James was right. When I got real with myself—when I accepted the fact that sometimes shit happens and I wouldn't always make the sale no matter how hard I worked or how much I believed I was right—I became a better salesman.

Of all the reasons to tell the truth, the simplest and most obvious one is it's absurd to tell a lie because nobody cares about what you're lying about, so it's easier and far less stressful to tell the damn truth in the first place.

I didn't graduate college; no big deal, because in the modern business climate, having a degree doesn't make or break you. I wasn't embarrassed by not having the sheepskin, but that didn't stop me from telling everybody that I went to Florida State, without mentioning that I didn't finish.

When I interviewed to get on *The Apprentice*, however, I was *very* up front about my lack of degree, because I knew that they could find out the truth in six seconds with a single email.

On the first day of filming, immediately after we walked into the boardroom and sat down at the conference table, Trump said something along the lines of, "This year's going to be different: Half of you have a college degree and half of you do not."

Uh-oh. My first thought: *Holy shit, I'm about to get outed to everybody that knows me, and there's nothing I can do about it. I can't believe this has happened.* This bothered me for my entire tenure on the show, but what could I do?

I was freaking out that when the show aired and it was revealed that I'd been bullshitting about college for years, I'd get crushed. But... *nothing*. Silence. Crickets. I never heard a word about it. Nobody gave a damn.

The takeaway from that particular story was that if you publicly perpetuate a non-truth—if you're hiding behind something that's not true in order to maintain your image—there's a strong chance that you shouldn't have lied in the first place, because nobody gives a shit.

But *you* give a shit. So be freakin' honest.

CHAPTER 2

THE ULTIMATE PARTNERSHIPS

MENTORS, MENTEES, SPOUSES, AND ASKHOLES

There's a phrase I heard a million years ago, and it's always stuck with me: *If you want to go fast, go alone. If you want to go far, go with others.* If you're a businessperson, take that to heart, because whether it's a mentor–mentee situation or a joint venture partnership, having a like-minded, simpatico individual by your side doesn't suck.

I've had dozens of partnerships throughout my personal and professional life. One of the keys to success is to look for people who haven't always been successful. Let me clarify: I want people who have experienced both success and failure. For instance, let's look no further than my current home of Las Vegas.

The worst thing that could ever happen to anybody on their first trip to Vegas is to win big on the first game they play. This happened to my sister the first time I ever taught her how to play craps on a riverboat casino in Shreveport, Louisiana. Quite frankly, she just couldn't lose, and after scraping up her winnings, she looked at me and said, "We should do this every weekend."

Me, having taken my lumps many times, explained to her, "That's not really the way this works, because the point is you learn more from losing than you do from winning; you learn more of what *does* work by finding out what *doesn't* work."

This is why people who actually understand gambling don't play roulette.

Anyhow, anytime you have multiple people working together toward a common goal, it's a partnership. (I don't care if it's your wife and your common goal is to raise your kids—that's a partnership. Honestly, your spouse/boyfriend/girlfriend/partner is the most important partnership you'll ever form, because if you choose the wrong mate, you're going to have a hard life, especially when you add children to the mix.) It could be said that the business equivalent of marriage is the mentor–mentee relationship. If you nail that one, you have a considerably better chance of succeeding in the business world… and a considerably better shot at keeping The Drift at bay.

If you're the mentee, you've got to find somebody who takes enough of an interest in you that they want to see you do well. For your part, you have to respect what advice the mentor has to offer… *then follow the damn advice*. The mentors I've had in my life are guys who've made millions, and lost millions, and have done the things that could potentially screw you up. So when you ask them for that advice, don't blow it off.

The first rule of being a good mentee: Don't be an askhole.

Not an asshole. An askhole.

We all have askholes in our lives. For instance, let's say your buddy calls you up and says, "John, I've got a problem."

After he lays out his issue, you might say, "That exact same thing happened to me two years ago and I fixed it *this way*, and I learned that the only way on the planet to fix this is to do it *this way*, so I know from painful personal experience that doing it *this way* is what you need to do."

They might say, "Yeah. Okay. That sounds good," then do the exact opposite thing.

That's an askhole. Let me break it down.

Several years back, a couple of real estate agents told me, "We want you to mentor us, to teach us how to build a team."

Admittedly, I *love* being a mentor, so I said, "Yes. Absolutely. I'll schedule a standing appointment with you guys once a week."

The first couple of weeks were fine—they asked the right questions and seemed to take the answers to heart. Then, two hours before our third meeting, I got a text message from one of them: "Hey, we have to cancel for this week. Something came up."

I thought, *No problem. Things come up.*

The next week, another text: "Hey. OMG, my partner can't make it. Can we reschedule for tomorrow?"

I texted back, "Don't take this in a condescending way, and don't take this in a hyper egotistical way, but here's a question for you: If you had a meeting with a high-profile business leader you admire, would you cancel it?"

He texted back, "No."

I wrote, "The reason you wouldn't have canceled is because you value the information that he would give you so much that it would never, ever even cross your mind to blow off an appointment with him. If you don't value my time in the same way, that means you don't value the information I'm giving you in the same way, which means you're never going to take my advice anyway. So this has just become a waste of all of our time."

If they don't take what you're saying to heart, there's no reason to say it.

When you get older and wiser, the thing you become most knowledgeable about—at least in my mind—is how much time you have left on this earth, so the value of your time goes up exponentially. When you're twenty, you believe you're going to live forever; you think you're immortal. But then when you get older, when you hit middle age, you start doing scary math: *The average life expectancy of a man is seventy-eight, and eighty-two for a woman. I'm already fifty years old, which means I've got about twenty-eight years left on the planet. I sleep eight hours a day, so that knocks off a third of my remaining hours. So I don't feel like sitting here giving you advice for an hour if you're not going to take it.*

A big part of taking advice is *remembering it*, so anytime your mentor speaks, make sure you *write it down*. A mentor may tell you something twice, but there's zero chance they're going to tell you three times. And if you ask them to, they probably won't tell you anything else ever again.

Another factor in a successful relationship is adding value. This is one of the most important things about getting what you want: learning to position the ask. To that end, just like all high-level entrepreneurs, I've had dozens of people reach out to me and say, "I'll come work for you for free. I'll do it for six months. I just want to be around you. I just want to come and be in your office. You don't have to pay me."

When it was a new thing, that approach often worked—foodies everywhere are aware that young and/or inexperienced chefs worked at Thomas Keller's restaurants for free—but in today's business climate, not so much. If you want to come work for somebody, whether for free or for a six-figure salary, you have to bring something to the table other than enthusiasm.

A better approach would be to say, "I've watched your career, and I'm trying to model mine after yours. I know that you're in a place where you're really trying to push forward, and it would mean everything to me if I could just come be your shadow...and it'll be worth your while because I believe that I could bring X, Y, and Z to the table."

Now you position the ask in a way that there's something in it for me. Now I have a reason to say yes. Now I'm motivated to teach. And bear in mind that I'm not looking for somebody to do my work for free—I want to hang out with somebody who's compelled to collaborate rather than go to school. A win for them, a win for me. That's partnership.

I'm in several mastermind groups, one of which is called the Boardroom, a group of the best real estate flippers, developers, wholesalers, and creative finance people. I flip myself, and I can sure as hell break down how to structure and scale a business, but I had no clue about creative finance. In my main business of opening partnered title companies, I don't get much business from the Boardroom, but I learn and they teach, and I teach and they learn, and that's a fulfilling transaction for everybody.

Here's another example, this one from 2006, when I first moved to Vegas, and the real estate market was falling apart, and everybody was talking about "short sales." Simply put, a short sale is when you negotiate with a bank and sell your product for less than it's worth.

Enter Lee Honish.

I saw an ad for a seminar that Lee was giving that said, basically, "I was a loss mitigator for a big bank, and I know everything about how to get short sales done. Come to my seminar." So I went, and holy shit, it was terrible. His presentation was bad, his stage presence was bad, his flow of information was bad, his pitch was bad...but I still saw a shit-ton of value in his well of knowledge.

I sent him an email the next day: "Lee, I was at your presentation yesterday, and I saw your product, and I'm not going to buy it, and here's why I'm not going to buy it." Then I laid out all the reasons why his presentation sucked and added, "The reason I can say that, to be blunt, is because I've sold millions of dollars in real estate from a stage. I'm a veteran at seminar sales and I know how to do that like the back of my hand. So I want you to come to Vegas, and we're going to spend half the day where you personally teach me everything you know about short sales, and then we'll spend the other half revamping your entire pitch, and I'll teach you how to sell from the stage. We can share each other's knowledge and we'll both benefit." That wasn't a partnership in the traditional sense of the word, nor was it a mentor–mentee relationship, because we'd be mentoring each other.

Two days later, Lee was in Las Vegas. I don't know how much he used onstage of what we developed in that room, but he definitely found value... and so did I.

Actually, I found a *lot* of value: The information I gleaned from him made me at least a million bucks.

This is wisdom I'm trying to impart upon my children. I'm friendly with the Vegas-based guys who founded the virtual fitness training company V Shred, a business that scored $200 million worth of sales in 2022. We were discussing my kids; specifically about how, when they hit a certain age, they start ignoring you. Nothing you say is going to resonate with them, and they think you're an idiot, and that's just how it is. So the V Shred guys agreed to let my then sixteen-year-old son intern with them, which I loved, because he was going to be around these young, hip guys... who happen to pull down $200 mil' a year. And the V Shred team was happy to do it, because they like me and some of the ideas that I happen to spout. Again, win-win.

Whenever I hire somebody to come work on my team, it's a mentor–mentee relationship. That being the case, the first questions I ask them are, "Where do you want to go? And what do you want to do?"

Some of those people say, "I just want to work for you. I want to close deals and I want to be happy here forever."

Okay, cool, fair enough. Landing a *forever job* is a legitimate goal.

Other people are like, "I want to be you—or some version of you—and have my own team, my own company, my own brokerage."

Totally different approach.

Thing is, if I don't know where you're trying to get to, if I don't know what your end goal is. I don't even want to start with you, because how I mentor you is going to be different based on your envisioned future, and if you don't have an envisioned future, there isn't much I can offer you.

You need to be able to articulate exactly—or almost exactly—where you're trying to go. If you're one of those people who wants to be a shadow or an intern, you should be able to articulate your goals beyond, "I want to eventually become part of your organization." You need to go a step further and say something like, "I'm going to bring enough value that I'll become part of your organization and help the organization continue to grow," then explain *how* you'll enable growth. Now, once you've gained a certain level of skill sets by following the advice of mentors, you're ready for the next type of partnership: a joint venture.

A joint venture partnership is when you have a distinct skill set and you find somebody else who has a complementary set of skills, and/or a similar business vision, and you tell them, "We should partner because, together, we can go further." (There's that African proverb again.) If both people have the *exact* same skill set, one of said people isn't required.

Too many business newbies want to find a partner because they're too scared to take the step by themselves—they just want somebody to hold their hand. (Seriously, if you want somebody to hold your hand, get a girlfriend or a boyfriend, or a professional hand-holder, or listen to a Beatles record.) But if you get a business partner just because you're frightened to take a step by yourself, *you're likely going to fail.*

If you're great at sales, find somebody who's great at numbers. If you're a forest guy (you dig the big picture), find somebody who loves dealing with the trees (they dig the nuts and bolts). To an extent, you want the opposite version of yourself, because if you and your partner agree on everything, that's not a partnership. That's a feedback loop.

For instance:

I spend a lot of time around some of the best digital marketers in the world, one of whom is a good friend by the name of Josh Aven. Josh handles about $100 million in annual digital ad spending for some of the biggest brands on the planet.

In the past I have developed several pieces of technology in the real estate space and, looking back and being honest, I can say all of these projects failed because I lacked the digital marketing experience to get them the exposure they needed to be successful.

Talking with Josh one night, it dawned on me that he could very easily complete the puzzle and help me launch a coaching program through an app. When I approached him with the idea, Josh said, "I can do that in my sleep."

Now, I'm a smart guy, but I don't have the ability to market on Josh's level...but I do have the industry knowledge required to get it going. By the time you're reading this book, our complementary skill sets will likely have led to a successful partnership.

There are different ways to build a joint venture, and the methods change as your business evolves. Let's say you're a decent salesperson. What you need to do—and this may sound super-simple, but people don't always realize it—is *find something to sell*. Let's call this the Tony Soprano Corollary.

Douglas James, an online marketing guru, told the story about his favorite approach on my podcast, also called *Escaping the Drift*. When I asked if he had to start again with zero what would he do, he responded by saying he would start over exactly the way he began. His first client was a limo company in a small town called Escondido, California. He found them by looking on the second page of Google where they were placed. Now everybody knows that if you're not on the first page of Google, chances are your business isn't exactly booming. Without telling them he was doing it, he set up a landing page and started marketing for Escondido Limo Service. He forwarded all the calls that came in from the new landing page directly to the limo service. After a few days, he called the owner and asked them, "Have you been busy?"

To which the owner replied, "We've been slammed."

After explaining to the owner what had happened, and that Douglas was responsible for their newfound windfall, the owner was happy to give up a percentage of his sales to keep the business flowing. And if he didn't pay? Douglas would've shut down his ads and landing page and took his business somewhere else. He essentially opened a limo company, with no limos and no drivers, only a keyboard.

The Tony Soprano Corollary. Straight-up baller. Bada-bing, bada-boom, fuhgeddaboudit.

One thing Tony didn't know about was the three-legged stool and why you should beware of it.

When I first got into the brokerage-owning business, I was going to leave my existing company, RE/MAX, and open a Keller Williams franchise, in part because my friend Kendra Todd—who'd won my season of *The Apprentice*—had recently gone to that company.

I flew to the Keller Williams mother ship in Austin, where I had dinner with Gary Keller. The meeting was fantastic, but I was nervous about making the jump. The husband-and-wife-owned company where I currently worked had a notorious reputation of going nuclear when people left their business. Bear in mind that this was at the time when bank relationships and foreclosure listings were very big business for those of us lucky enough to have them—and this company was infamous for taking people's money. It was bad.

In order to keep the nuclear explosion at bay, I offered them a percentage of my new business, just so they wouldn't mess with me. When it came time to deliver the news, Mr. Nuclear was out of town, so I told Mrs. Nuclear, "I'll give you 5 percent of my new venture just to let me go clean."

Soon after that, I went back to Austin to firm up the deal with Gary. That night, I was standing at a bar with my buddy, and I got a phone call from one of my agents. "Hey, John," he said, "there're two armed guards here. They won't let us into the office."

"What?"

Right then, my phone pinged an email notification. It was Mr. Nuclear, telling me that I was fired, and wasn't allowed back on the premises.

Luckily, before this process started, I had called all the banks that housed my foreclosure accounts and warned them, "These people have this notorious reputation. This could get sticky." Very soon thereafter, the Nuclear family called the banks and said, "We had to terminate Gafford because we found out he was misappropriating money. But we'll be happy to keep the account with you."

I had to get back to business immediately, because I was going to lose all these very lucrative bank accounts, and if that came to pass, the agents on my team would probably scatter to the wind. So I called the regional guy for Keller Williams and gave him the skinny.

He was totally unfazed. "Another Keller Williams franchise by me has some office space. You can move in and incubate."

By Monday morning, I had those offices painted and decorated, and my agents' computers were set up and ready to go. And those agents, loyal as ever, walked into work like nothing had happened. One of them even pulled me aside and said, "Wow, man, this is really impressive that you did this."

I said, "The time is now. I don't screw around."

That same day, one of the partners of the KW franchise where I was temporarily working came to me and said, "We have three partners here, and one of them is not doing that much. For that matter, he's not doing *anything*. Why don't you just buy him out, and become our partner here, and we'll open a second franchise together?"

Which is exactly what I did. Inside of eighteen months, we had two offices that were staffed by 180-plus agents, a whopping 400 percent more agents than when I showed up.

Good stuff. But not perfect.

The two partners had been best friends for years, so I became the third leg on the stool. Seemingly every decision that required a vote led to a two-to-one loss, them being the two and me being the one. The takeaway from that was, if you're going to partner with more than one other person, you'd better go into it with an absolute understanding of what everybody's role is, of what everybody is supposed to do, of where their responsibility and decision-making begins and ends. You should probably also have a really good understanding of the other partners' relationships, because if you're the third drummer to join the band after the previous two were canned, well, suffice it to say that just because you're playing on the record doesn't mean you're going to be touring with the group.

Now this is not to say that you can't be in a partnership with more than one person. Streamline, our mortgage company, has three partners. I don't know that this relationship would be as successful as it is had I not had the disaster at Keller Williams. I'm constantly aware of everyone's position and how decision-making affects not just the business but the psychology of all the partners. The key to this is empathy. Never make a decision in a partnership without considering not only the position of your partners, but how the outcome will affect them as people.

The Keller Williams deal was a nasty situation, obviously, but on the plus side, I did learn a few other lessons, the biggest one being that before launching into any partnership—mentor–mentee, husband–wife, joint venturer–joint venturer—look for red flags *everywhere*. One of the reddest flags often comes from people who get too close to you, too quickly.

Right now my business partner is Gavin Ernstone, and I love Gavin. I think he's a wonderful human being, but he's not my best friend. He lives a mere twenty minutes from my house, but we rarely socialize beyond work. Sure, we'll do one or two dinners a year, and sure, we go to lunch, and we talk on the phone almost every day, but maintaining a little bit of distance has allowed us to make some money together while remaining very good work-friends. If we got too embroiled in each other's lives, I think it would create problems.

Different partnerships, different rules.

Partnering with family can have its pitfalls, and if you don't have a strong relationship with the relative in question, a deal that goes sideways can fracture your bond beyond repair. Fortunately, I have a very strong relationship with my sister Nicole, and I say fortunately because we got into some shit that went as sideways as it could go.

Back when I was working at the car dealership, Nicole was the COO for an individual who headed up one of the biggest Amway organizations in the country. Their territory was half of the United

States and all of England, as well as some other foreign countries. Nicole, who's very, very bright, called me up one day and said, "We're going to start a multi-level marketing business and we're going to sell supplements."

Like I said, Nicole is very, very bright, so, without hesitation, I said, "Awesome."

Now multi-level marketing companies—aka, MLMs—can be iffy ventures, but I was selling cars, so that didn't faze me one bit. Sure, I was earning my PhD in sales, and sure, I knew nothing about supplements—or, for that matter, multi-level marketing—but if there's a potentially great opportunity that comes my way, I'm jumping at it. No Drifting for John Gafford.

When I told my old pal Rick Wells about the company, he mentioned the possibility of bringing in high-profile athletes to support the launch—including a few he had personal connections with.

Rick was still VP at WorldCom, and in terms of his investments, he had zero diversity—his 401(k) and all his stock options were all WorldCom, all the time. Then, one day, the company imploded because they'd been faking their accounting *forever*, Enron-style, and Rick's portfolio went to zero. He lost his job, his savings, *everything*.

Naturally, he went into an absolute dark place... and this was right before we were about to launch the supplement company. For weeks, I'd call him up and say, "Okay, time to go, time to go, time to go."

He wouldn't even leave his bed. I couldn't get him to do anything.

My sister and I had gambled so much of this enterprise on the ability of one of our partners to deliver something that was pivotal to the success of the business, and he failed. I couldn't get *too* angry at him. Not too many people would've been able to bounce back from something like that quickly. But it still hurt.

None of this impacted my relationship with Nicole. Business is business, but family is family.

The big lesson there was, if you're all in on a business, your operational partners also have to be all in. Sure, there'll be plenty of financial partners who want to invest and be hands off, saying stuff like, "I'm going to give you money. I believe in your concept. We'll give you the bread, now go do your thing." But if you're depending on somebody to show up, they need to show up, and if they're not going to, you need to move on from them ASAP.

And that was our mistake. We put all our eggs in one basket, and that basket ended up failing miserably.

Eagerness is oftentimes a great motivator. If you meet somebody who's obsessed with performing—and who's nowhere near The Drift—it might not be a bad idea to make a move.

To wit, one afternoon I was sitting in my office, minding my own literal and figurative business, when a gentleman from the huge mortgage company Movement Mortgage burst in. He explained that he worked for something called Core Service Partners, a branch of their business that creates joint venture partnership title companies with large brokerages. He said, "You guys aren't going to have to do anything. We're going to handle everything. We're invested. You come aboard, we'll do a joint venture and we'll get rich." Then he proceeded to explain how it would all work.

Capping off your presentation with "We'll get rich," then laying out specific plans on how to do so isn't a bad way to end a pitch. I said, "Okay, great."

It wasn't great. At least at first.

Early on, there was a lot of disinterest, which I surmised was rooted in the fact that this business might've been Movement Mortgage's redheaded stepchild. Their attitude seemed to be, *We'll see if it works, but if it doesn't, it was underfunded anyhow, so no great loss.*

Very quickly, we realized this was a problem.

Everything was a pain in the ass, but eventually, sure enough, we started making money. But the vibe was so negative that I kept thinking, *God, I hate this business, but man, we made a hundred grand last month. How do we shut this down?*

And then one Thursday, I got an email from Core Service Partners Corporate. This email was a massive screwup on their part—it wasn't supposed to go to me. Turns out they'd mistakenly sent me a spreadsheet listing all of their joint partnerships. And on their spreadsheet was how much—or how little—each company was bringing in.

Each and every one of them was losing money. We were the only one that had turned a profit—and a big profit at that. Naturally, I give them a jingle.

Without preamble, I said, "Guys, look, we're doing all the work. We're earning all the money. So we're buying you out."

If you have a viable business—something that's working well—as soon as you identify that you have the wrong partner, shut it down. If it's not the right person or people, you've got to get them out of the way. And if you can make a profit off of moving on from that partner, so much the better—but in some instances, it's worth getting out of a shitty partnership even if it *is* making you money. After all, keeping a high level of happiness and holding on to your sanity isn't a bad thing.

Sometimes something you think isn't a partnership actually *is* a partnership, and a good one at that. That sounds weird, but stick with me here.

Some of the best partnerships I've ever had are with people who work for me. It's not a mentor–mentee relationship, mind you, but rather a boss–employee one. Even if they're an employee, we're still working together toward a common goal, so, by definition, we're partners.

I realized that in my early twenties when I was working in management at Hooters. And get your mind out of the gutter. It was strictly business. Most of the time, anyway.

I quickly rose through the Hooters ranks, becoming a general manager. The only caveat was that my first assignment as a general manager was the absolute worst store in the entire company, a piece of shit outside St. Louis. I guess they figured that, worst-case scenario, I couldn't screw it up any worse.

My assistant was a guy named Dave Levins, and we clicked instantly. From the get-go, we were Jordan and Pippen, hitting each other on the fast break, then finishing with a slam. We both had what the other one lacked, and it worked out idyllically, and here's why: I invested my time dealing with the business side of things, while Dave handled the people. Now I'm a people person, and nobody there disliked me, but my goodness, they *loved* Dave. As long as I could get him to embed our plans and concepts in the workforce's collective brain, and get everybody aligned on our standards, we were good.

So good, in fact, that in a mere eight months, that restaurant became the most improved profit location in the country, from worst to first. Dave and I were the comeback kids, and they started shipping us to every problem restaurant they had. I'd get calls from the president of the company and at first when he said, "I need a favor," I would respond with, "What?"

I learned very quickly to change my answer to, "Where?"

From that point on, I dragged Dave every place I went; when they made me a multi-store supervisor, I insisted that Dave be the GM of the worst store in the region. He got so good at cleaning up the shittiest stores—and he was happy to do it—that I sent him to, well, all the shittiest stores. He never complained, and he always kicked ass. Even post-Hooters, I hired him to work for me again and again. That, right there, is the ideal partnership, the kind of partnership that will absolutely stave off The Drift.

CHAPTER 3

THERE'S ALWAYS AN OUT

YOU CAN DO ANYTHING, AND WHEN I SAY ANYTHING, I MEAN *ANYTHING*

If you Drift, you're probably quite familiar with admitting defeat. Maybe you've thrown in the towel once. Or maybe twice. Or maybe thirty-seven times. Maybe you gave up on a job because it got too hard. Maybe you ended a romance because it got too *real.* Maybe you threw out the skeleton of an unfinished Ikea bookcase because it got too difficult to use the Allen wrench.

If you're Drifting now, or have done so in the past, chances are *very* good that at some point in your life, you gave up on something.

To some, not giving up seems simple. For them, all they need to say is, "I'm not giving up," and they don't give up. But not everybody is built that way. To that end, let's talk about health. Specifically, obesity.

An overweight person might try to diet for a month, then, after losing just three pounds, say, "Welp, it's genetic. I'm predisposed to being overweight."

I don't want to hear that. I've seen too many television shows with titles along the lines of *America's Worst Baker*, and I've never seen any of the contestants take responsibility for their messed-up cheesecakes. And that's unfortunate, because they absolutely have the power to fix their sweet treats.

The good news is that just because you might not be *built* that way doesn't mean you have to *stay* that way.

Many tend to think that the easiest thing in the world to do when adversity strikes—when you get metaphorically punched in the mouth—is to say, *This is beyond fixing. I'm stuck.*

Wrong. *There's always an out.* That's a fact. Thus the name of the chapter.

The quickest way to escape this aspect of The Drift is to look at your problems as just that—problems. They're not curses. They're not lifetime sentences. They're problems, and problems, by definition, have solutions. If you can change your mindset from *victim* to *fixer*, from *complainer* to *solution seeker*, from *pessimist* to *optimist*, from *hater* to *lover*, you can dig your way out. Your instinct, upon getting hit with adversity, should always be, *How can I make this better*, rather than, *Holy crap, life sucks.*

I've said it before, and I'll say it again: *Don't let the world happen to you. You happen to the world.*

If you're a parent like me, you nip this in the bud with your children, as negativity can be passed down from generation to generation. If you create a dark household, you and your family might gravitate toward darkness, thus gravitating toward Drifting.

The Gafford household is sure as shit not a negative household.

Young children don't always see solutions...and why should they? That's not their job. But as they grow into adolescence and young adulthood, they have to start learning how to fix their own problems.

For example, as I write this, my son is pulling straight A's. (That's always been one of his goals, which continues to impress me. The kid is amazing—like genius level—when it comes to academics. Truth be told, he gets that from his mother.) He was given an assignment for which he was supposed to read a book. Unfortunately, he forgot to get the book in question. Distraught, he told me, "I'm going to get a bad grade, and it's going to bring me down to a B."

I said, "Well, what are you going to do about it?"

"There's nothing I can do."

There're a couple of things you can't say at Chez Gafford, and *There's nothing I can do* is one of them, because, as noted, there's always an out.

I asked him, "Do you have the teacher's email address?"

"No, I don't."

"Can you get it?"

"Yeah, probably."

I said, "Okay, if you can get the teacher's email, I want you to send her a note. I want you to explain to her what happened and see if there's any way you can make this up. I want you to see if there's a solution."

He said, "That's not going to work."

"How do you know?"

"I just know."

"Do you have anything to lose by trying it?" I asked. "What's the worst that can happen?"

He shrugged and said, "Fine. I'll write it."

Some who face adversity aren't hardwired to deal with having a door slammed in their face. They don't want to hear *No* again because it compounds the problem...but you've got to be willing to take that risk.

Sure enough, the teacher answered his email almost immediately: "You're the best student I have in the class. I know the level at which you read. I know the books that you read are far beyond what we're assigning anyway. So you know what? Don't even worry about the assignment. Don't even worry about reading the book."

Fear of the word *No* in moments of adversity keeps many from looking for a way out. For example, as salespeople, being on the phone is a big part of what we do, because that's the best way to establish relationships and build businesses. These days, some folks don't like to work the phone in any type of sales situation because they're scared of the word *No*.

As for my son's Case of the Missing Book, what would've happened if the teacher said, "No book means a ding on your grade"? Would asking if there's a way to fix things at that point mean he's going to fail *more*? No. Asking will lead to a solution. It may not be the solution he's looking for, but at least the situation will be resolved. As it so happens, making the ask led to a perfect resolution, and it never would've come to pass had he not made the ask.

See? Nothing. To. Lose.

We're also instilling this sort of thing into our now fourteen-year-old daughter.

I tell people my son will probably go to an excellent school, and get a marvelous degree, and get a wonderful job working in a beautiful building... a building owned by my daughter. The girl operates like a gangster... and I mean that with nothing but love, admiration, and affection.

I'd like to think this all has something to do with the fact that I bestowed upon the kids the ownership of the vending machine at my company. It's been their business since about 2019. They do the accounting, they stock it (although their mother's the delivery driver), and stack it with singles, and any money they pull out of it belongs to them.

Naturally, most of the money comes in the form of dollar bills, which my daughter has always called "fat stacks." (How gangster is that?) Of my two kids, she's the saver, living in a bedroom filled with $2,000 in ones. (My son spends his money quickly, buying the latest version of whatever video game he's obsessed with at the time.) One day, when my daughter was nine, the cleaning ladies were coming over, and I needed small bills to tip them. I said to my daughter, "Do me a favor. Break this $100 for me."

She gave me a look and said, "No."

"What do you mean *no*?"

"I like my fat stacks."

After some back-and-forth, she finally agreed to give me the change. Thing is, she gave me $96 in small bills. I said, "You shorted me four bucks."

She shrugged and, without even looking up, said, "Service charge."

I said, "Excuse me?"

Then she looked up and said, "Would you rather go to the store to get change?"

Nine years old. And she was charging me juice. The kid is ruthless.

Anyhow, one day she came home from her Catholic school and told me, "I don't like the assigned seating at lunch. It's the only time I get to hang out with my friends, and none of them are at my table."

I said, "Well, what're you going to do about it? What can you do?"

Without so much as a pause or a thought, she said, "I'm going to write a letter."

Which is exactly what she did. And my goodness, that letter was well-crafted. She bullet-pointed her argument, saying that allowing students to choose their own seats would promote inclusion and be beneficial to the children and the teachers alike.

The next day, she handed it to the teacher, who, almost immediately, told her, "You're right. You can have open seating."

My kid affected change at her school just because she had the wherewithal to say, *I'm going to do everything in my power to try to fix this. And if I can't fix it, at least I'll go down swinging.* If you take that kind of attitude into your business—if you spray your energy and creativity toward the right thing—good things will happen. But not everybody knows how or where to spray. I find the main problem for people who don't see the way out simply comes down to focus.

Sometimes in business, people focus on the wrong things. They might think, *Big sales solve everything,* paying attention solely to the top line, like gross sales. The reality of it is, what's worth more than gross sales is *profitability,* because if a business is not profitable, it doesn't stay open. You can deliver the most impressive sales in the world, but if it costs a gazillion dollars to get those sales, you lose, and those kinds of losses might lead to a Drift. Focus on profitability because that's what'll keep your business moving forward.

But more important than any of that is your cash flow. If your business doesn't have flow, you won't have capital to keep it open. What I've found in most of the businesses for whom I consult is that they do, indeed, focus on the top line and profitability, but they're not heavily focused on cash flow. Bad idea, because little is more important to a business than what's in its bank account. Yeah, I know, this sort of multitasking is difficult—it takes plenty of effort to juggle sales, marketing, advertising, and sales force management—but it has to be done.

For example, say you're buying parts to build widgets at your widget factory. Whenever the delivery guy drops the supplies off at your factory, you've got to pay him on the spot; you've got to write him a check, and the second you write the check, that money is gone, and you won't see a return until you sell the widgets.

Which won't happen until after they're built and distributed.

Which might not happen for another six months.

Now you've got yourself a cash problem because you won't be getting the money back as fast as you paid it out. Whenever you're looking at any type of a business model, you have to make sure the money coming in is coming in as rapidly—or *more* rapidly—than the money going out.

The same thought process can be applied to your personal finances. Here's a life exercise that could crystallize this for you: Lose your credit card.

I don't mean to ditch it altogether; just misplace it and get a new one. Because, like most of us, you have a shit-ton of your bills set to autopay. With your replacement credit card in hand, you now have to go in and reenter that number everywhere you have a subscription, and you'll learn exactly what's going out. It'll force you to audit every single one of your subscriptions, and one thing you'll realize is that your financial problems aren't necessarily your giant bills—not the car payment, not the rent payment, not the mortgage payment. The problem is stuff like the twenty-five streaming services for which you drop a few hundred bucks each month.

I mean, do you really need HBO Max if all you watch is *Game of Thrones*?

It's those dozens of little paper cuts that bleed you to death. For instance, I was coaching somebody who'd been paying $29 a month for unlimited access to American Airlines Wi-Fi—*and he hadn't been on an American Airlines flight in two years.* That's almost $700, pissed away. If that's not some Drift-y shit, I don't know what is.

The power to change this sort of behavior is, again, all about focus, and I'll stand by that thesis so much that I'm offering you a money-back guarantee: If you audit your credit card statements and knock out subscriptions that you don't use, you'll save more than enough money to cover the cost of this book. If you don't, I'll send you a refund.

You're welcome.

There are dozens of ways to apply this sort of attitude and behavior to business, even with something as seemingly simple as your hiring practices.

I had a situation with one of our companies where we were using a recruiter we'd previously worked with when we were recruiting C-level executives. In this case, we needed somebody who *wasn't* a C-level employee, and they found us a person who we hired at a salary of $55,000 per year. After the I's were dotted and the T's were crossed with the new hire, the company quoted me a price of $11,000 for their services... something that may have been mentioned to a member of our company, but it certainly didn't get back to me.

I called them up and said, "Here's the deal: For that level of employee, I'm going to give you $2,000, because I know it couldn't have been that hard to find them since it wasn't a high-level thing. I value the relationship I have with you, but I'm only going to give you $2,000, and if you can't accept that, unfortunately, you're going to have to sue me. And I know it's going to cost you more than eleven grand to sue me."

A couple of days later, they came back and said, "We want our money. That's our fee. And you have to pay us our fee, because we earned it."

I said, "That's your opinion. Can you please take this up with somebody who can understand where we're at? I'm offering you $2,000 to settle it, and if you accept, I'll continue to use your business for our C-level stuff. Or you can hold me to this eleven grand—which I'm not paying anyway—and our relationship will be done, and you'll have lost a bunch of business from me." Sure enough, they realized that a long-term relationship was far more valuable, so they took the two grand.

I don't like to negotiate like that, but sometimes, unfortunately, as was the case in this instance, you have to. They didn't do anything wrong, per se; they just did what they always do. Truth be told, I was just taking a hard stance in the negotiation to see what I could get because, again, anytime you're negotiating, the person who seems like they want to walk away from the table is the person who usually wins. Negotiating is basically a form of asking somebody for something, and as we've learned from my kids, it never hurts to ask.

And if you ask and you don't get the answer you like, you ask again. I'm good at that because, well, I'm literally the best complainer in the entire world. It's a gift.

Here's how you, too, can be a superhero complainer.

If you're required to deal with any type of customer service—and if you call the 800 number, you've already lost—here's what you do: You look for the email format of the company and the corporate office, then you find out who the CEO is, then you write an email directly to them explaining your problem. Because if you get through to the CEO, magical things can happen.

After I get the proper contact information, I'll seek out the notes from the company's quarterly shareholder meetings and learn the terminology they use to describe their business so I can put it in my complaint.

If you do it right, it *will* work.

For instance, my wife is a Disney fanatic, so we've had season passes for a gazillion years. One day, I took the family to Disney to celebrate one of the kids' birthdays, and from the second we got to the park, something about this visit was *off*.

The hotel on the Disney property—*off*.

Goofy's Kitchen—*off*.

Space Mountain—*off*.

We were supposed to have a birthday party at the little restaurant off Main Street, and whoever was in charge didn't refrigerate our cupcakes, and it was so hot that the cupcakes melted.

Ordinarily, I'd let something like that go, but, man, it was a bunch of money we'd spent, so when we got home, I tracked down the notes from Disney's quarterly stockholders' meeting, where I learned that those of us who have season passes and stay at the hotels on the grounds are called "heavy users."

Keeping that in mind, I wrote a note to the CEO of Disney, as well as the VP at Disney Parks, laying out our shitty trip, how often we visit, and how much money we spend, and how we were long-time "heavy users."

Within an hour, I got a call.

"Hi, John, this is Brad from Disney. We just received your email, and we're very distraught. As a way to make it up to you and your family, we're going to send your kids a care package."

Sure enough, a few days later, we received a bunch of Disney swag, as well as a certificate for a three-day stay in a suite at the Disneyland Hotel, not to mention a three-day Park Hopper ticket.

Note that the email I wrote them wasn't scathing or angry—I simply laid out the facts using Disney-speak. The point is that sometimes when you ask, you can't *just* ask—you have to come to the table armed with facts and figures. If you do it right—if you go to the top in a polite, professional manner—magic can happen. Because Disney is a magical place.

Sometimes these sorts of problems are completely self-inflicted. But they can still be fixed.

One thing you need to do is get everything you can in writing, a lesson I learned when I was running the largest private German beer hall in Atlanta. For that matter, it was the largest beer hall in the entire Southeast. Almost immediately after I started, I realized that their concept was dated and sorely in need of a reboot. I went to the two owners and said, "Here's the deal: This needs to be changed, and that needs to be changed, and everything needs to be changed. I'm willing to change it all, but I want to be a partner in this." This turned out to be a three-legged stool at its worst. I'm not immune from it taking a few times for a lesson to sink in.

To their credit, one of them said, "Yeah, man, if you can make us money, sure."

I divided the venue into three establishments: a live music club called the Go Lounge, a Cajun restaurant called Bayou La Roux, and a Key West–themed bar called Clutch Cargo's. We were in the Buckhead section of Atlanta, so I dubbed the whole thing the Buckhead Block.

Very quickly, we started making a ton of money, and also very quickly, they received an offer from a national chain who, having seen what that space could net, wanted in. The owners accepted the offer, then cut me out... *because I never got my portion of ownership in writing*. I ended up settling with them for pennies on the dollar, which taught me that you have the power to ask someone to write it down, so use that power.

There are other paths you can take when trying to dig yourself out of a problem, one of those being the path of pure balls. So let's talk balls.

I was invited to an early-morning pitch meeting with a large private physician practice, and soon after I arrived, I found myself sitting at a table with twenty-four doctors in the midst of their monthly bull session. Right when I sat down, I realized I'd forgotten to bring a business card.

In today's post-COVID world, nobody gives a shit about business cards, but before that, if you didn't have a business card, you were an amateur.

After the meeting—which went exceedingly well—the group's alpha doctor said, "Great stuff, Mr. Gafford. We'll talk about it and get back to you. Do you have a card?"

Right then, I had two options: Tell him I forgot the card, or dive into my bag of tricks and find a way out. Even then, I knew there was always a way out, so I went with choice B.

In this case, "B" stood for "balls."

I looked the doctor in the eye and said, "Business cards are for dipshits that do callbacks. My contact information is on the bottom of the contract."

There was a moment of horrified silence, then many moments of hysterical laughter. The alpha doc said, "Well, I guess we'll need to see the contract."

Fortunately, I remembered to bring the contract, which I pulled out of my briefcase and slam-dunked on the table. Paper signed, deal done, problem quashed, Drift averted.

While that's a funny story, let's talk about something that isn't funny: Many Americans have a credit score that ranks in the fair to shitty category.

Fair to shitty is shitty.

Earlier in this chapter, I made a joke about all the weight loss shows on television. But quite frankly, shitty credit is a weight that's affecting you as much, if not more, than your waistline.

I've never weighed 400 pounds so I'm not going to sit here and tell you how to healthily get thin. I have, on the other hand, absolutely demolished my credit at one point in my life. When I was stuck in The Drift, I spent way too much time being a victim because of my credit score rather than taking charge of it.

Bad credit has real-life, day-to-day consequences. Back in my Drift days, I had no choice but to buy a beater car at a 20 percent interest rate, then was forced to hide said car from the repo man because I couldn't make the payments that were too high for me.

When it came to screwing up credit, my younger self was an absolute artist. I've felt the shame of walking out of a bank after being turned down for a checking account, so when it comes to the fallout from having bad credit, I get it. The sad truth of all of it is when I actually decided to *do* something about it, it wasn't that big of a deal to fix—it just took focus, time, and a plan.

If your credit is bad—or you have what seems to be an insurmountable amount of debt—you have to take charge of that *today*. There are so many credit repair companies that can help you that it just makes no sense not to do this. Stop trying to climb an unclimbable mountain and meet with a reputable bankruptcy attorney and start over. If you think you can't afford either of these options, I assure you that you're paying more than this anytime you fill out an application that asks for your credit. Stop Drifting in financial ruin, and start swimming toward financial security.

All of which reminds me of something Lee Atwater once said: "When your opponent is drowning, you throw them a brick." The problem with people stuck in The Drift is that when they're drowning, they tend to *grab* a brick. By understanding that you always have a solution, you can avoid grabbing bricks and start grabbing life rafts.

CHAPTER 4

GAMING THE SYSTEM AND READING THE UNWRITTEN RULES

KICKING ASS AT MONOPOLY

Do you want to win every game of Monopoly you play for the rest of your life, while simultaneously driving your game-playing friends and family crazy? Of course you do. Here's how:

- Beg, borrow, steal, or trade away your financial future in order to acquire as many two- or three-property sets as possible.
- After securing that monopoly, load each property with houses. Not hotels. Houses.
- When you have four houses on each property—the maximum number of houses allowed, according to the game rules—do nothing.

Logic would dictate that once you get your four houses, you trade in the houses and buy yourself a hotel, because hotel rent is pricier than the maximum house rent. Thing is, Boardwalk with four houses will set your opponent back $1,700, while the hotel fee is $2,000, and $300 isn't that big of a deal when you have the option of cornering the entire housing market.

You see, once all thirty-two houses included with the game are in play, there's a housing shortage, and when there's a housing shortage, *nobody else in the game can build a damn thing*. No houses mean no hotels. Yes, that'll slow the game down considerably, but if you wait everybody out, *boom*, you win.

That may seem like you're bending the rules, but you're not—you're simply *understanding* the rules and using them to suit your needs. Think about it: There's nowhere in the Monopoly rule book that says a player is allowed to use something to replace the plastic properties, meaning, in my mind, once they're gone, they're gone. Knowing that, you can use the rules in your favor, and when the rules work for you, you have a considerably better chance to push away The Drift.

I'm not the only guy who utilizes the rule book to his favor. Author Tim Ferriss was far from a kickboxer, but that didn't stop him from trying to succeed at this ridiculously difficult sport.

In 1999, he won the gold medal at the Chinese Kickboxing National Championships.

Tim said it wasn't because he was good at punching and kicking. He won by reading the rules and looking for loopholes, of which he found two. First, weigh-ins were the day prior to competition. He lost twenty-eight pounds in eighteen hours (due to purposeful dehydration), weighed in at 165 pounds, after which he rehydrated back up to 193 pounds. Second, there was a technicality in the fine print (of the rule book). If one combatant fell off the elevated platform three times in a single round, his opponent won by default. Tim decided to use this technicality as his single technique and just push people off. The result? Tim won all his matches by TKO and went home as National Champion, something 99 percent of those with five-to-ten years of experience had been unable to do.

Tim read the rules, and he understood the rules, and he used them to suit his needs.

This sort of sideways approach can work in venues outside the Monopoly board and kickboxing ring, specifically in a high school or a college, where it can help you (almost) always get an A on a subjective paper.

When it comes to testing, there's black-and-white stuff, material that has concrete answers. If you're plowing through a multiple-choice Scantron page, and you fill in a C when the answer is D, you're just wrong. Subjective papers—papers propelled by opinions—are a different animal altogether.

What you have to realize is that teachers are among the most overworked, underpaid people in the world, and their time is unbelievably valuable, something that you can use to your advantage. If you're not happy with your B grade on a paper called, oh, I don't know, how about "Why Selling Real Estate Is the Greatest Profession in the World," head over to your professor's office after hours and ask for an explanation as to why you didn't get an A.

The professor will likely give you a three-to-five-minute breakdown as to why your work didn't meet their standards. Whatever they tell you, say, "I don't understand. Can you explain it to me again?"

They'll give you another two minutes. Listen politely, then ask again. And again. And again. After you've burned an hour of their time, tell them, "I think I get what you're saying. I'm really glad to know that if this happens again, you'll again be willing to spend this kind of time with me."

The professor won't change the grade on the paper you just spent an hour discussing, but you can confidently believe that next time they see your name on a page, they're going to think, *If I give this kid a B, he's going to come back in here and tie me up for an hour*, and if they're sitting on the fence, unable to decide your grade, they'll likely lean toward an A because they don't want to ever see you in their office again.

That bit of advice has worked at every level of education I've ever had, the lesson being that gaming the rules without being dishonest or straight-up shitty can be a fantastic anti-Drift mechanism. That said, I've found that people stuck in The Drift rarely pay attention to the rules they should be playing by, be they written or unwritten. Which is why it's the ideal time to discuss The Pen.

The Pen stemmed from an excerpt from my podcast that I posted on social media. In the clip, I told a story about how my friend Eric, when he's out with a big group at a restaurant, always does this thing when the server takes the group's order by memory. He'll pleasantly say, "Do you want to get a pen? I'm happy to wait." If they decline, he'll add, "Okay, but if something comes out wrong, I don't have to tip you. Fair?"

At that point, they'll always stop and go get The Pen. *Always.*

This post blew up to the tune of hundreds of thousands of views and tens of thousands of comments, running the gamut from, "Hell, yeah, Gafford!" to "I'd spit on that customer's plate."

Now understand that I've done every job in that sector of the service industry, so I'm speaking from experience when I say that, generally speaking, there are three types of people you'll find serving tables at a restaurant:

1. Professional waiters.
2. Those studying to do something else.

3. People stuck in The Drift.

Back when I waited tables, I was #3. And I was a no-pen-do-it-by-memory guy. Looking back, I realize that I blew off The Pen so the people sitting at my tables—who I'd likely never see again—wouldn't think I was dumb. (Now I'm aware that they never considered my intelligence. The No Pen trick was simply an ego boost.)

The Pen brings up some questions.

Q: Why do you go to work?
A: To make money.

Q: How do you make money waiting tables?
A: Tips.

Q: What drives good tips?
A: Proper service and making sure the guest has a great experience.

Q: Where does having an excellent memory fit into that equation?
A: It doesn't.

Q: When was the last time you recommended a restaurant to a friend and cited the amazing memory of the waitstaff?
A: I never have.

The Pen is the best insurance policy waiters have to protect their own income, yet so many play a different game with different rules, the kind of rules that will keep them Drifting along.

Restaurants offer masterclasses in unwritten rules, but if you're an excellent server—or chef, or line cook, or host—you'll have enough leverage to write your own rules, a fact that you can apply to virtually any professional situation. For example, during my stint at the car dealership, I quickly became one of their top salesmen; nonetheless, I was miserable. Yeah, I was good at selling cars—really good—but there's no way I was going to do it forever.

After I felt I'd earned my PhD in sales, per Rick Wells's advice, I decided to move back to Florida. I lied to my boss as to why I was leaving, telling him, "I'm gonna quit because all four of my roommates moved out, and I'm going to move back to Florida." I don't know why I didn't give him the full blow-by-blow. But I was young, so what're you gonna do?

Sean, my boss, said, "You can't afford your rent."

"Correct."

Sean nodded and said, "Here's what I'm gonna do. I'll be your roommate."

"Huh?" That was a twist.

"Yeah, I'll be your roommate, and I'll be the best roommate you've ever had. You had four roommates, so I'll pay four-fifths of your bills, and I'll never step foot in the house, and you'll be paying the exact same rent."

I realized in the moment that because I was selling so many cars and making Sean so much money, it was worth it for him to do whatever he could to keep me. But I still refused his offer, which, truth be told, was a damn good offer.

This proves that if you follow the rule *When it comes to your job, make yourself indispensable*, good things will likely happen. And I say *likely* because that coin has a flip side: If you're good at what you do—or, more accurately, good at *teaching* others what you do—you might just be making yourself *very* dispensable.

That particular factoid came crashing down on my head during my tenure at the Cobalt Lounge.

Back in 2000, in the aftermath of a fight two blocks down the street from Cobalt Lounge that featured Baltimore Ravens linebacker Ray Lewis, Lewis was charged with double homicide. After that incident, Cobalt's sales fell off dramatically, so much so that the owners of the club had to cut costs. I was just about the biggest expense on the books, so when it came time to clean house, they kept one of my lower-paid mentees on staff... a mentee who was ready to replace me... *because I taught him everything he needed to know about running the place.*

Years later, I saw an interview with Dwayne "The Rock" Johnson, in which he related a quote from his father: "I taught you everything that *you* know, but I didn't teach you everything that *I* know."

An unwritten rule of the corporate world is, *Make sure your subordinates are completely up to speed,* but when somebody else can control whether you have a job or not, you need to heed The Rock's father's advice. Bring your team up to a place where they can support you in the best possible way, but not to the point where they can replace you.

All that said, understand that rules can be changed by the people in charge of the domain in question. To illustrate, let's revisit my illustrious career at Hooters.

My first Hooters assignment was in Melbourne, Florida, a sleepy little beach town south of Daytona. When I first rolled into the restaurant, the other assistant manager, whose name was Chris, pulled me aside and said, "Let me tell you how you do it in Melbourne. When you work in a kind of outpost like this, the chances of you running into somebody from corporate are pretty slim. You might see your area supervisor once every two weeks, and they usually announce when they're coming."

Noted.

The next morning—which, mind you, was my second day in Melbourne—Chris called in. "I'm sick," he said with a sniffle. "Can you cover for me tonight? I'm closing, so you'll need to stay the whole day."

"Sure." I have no issues with somebody staying home with an illness. If you're sick, you're sick.

Early that evening, our area supervisor strolled in for a surprise visit.

The guy—whose name was, I shit you not, Guy—was there to check on me, and that's fair; I was new, and he *should've* checked on me. Normally, that wouldn't be an issue, as I'm happy to mingle with the higher-ups, but Chris was at home, possibly vomiting, possibly coughing up a lung, possibly burning up with a fever. It would've been nice to present a united front.

After some pleasantries, Guy looked around and asked, "Where's Chris?"

"He's at home, sick."

Guy nodded. "Sick, eh? Really? Okay, give me his number."

After dialing him up, Guy didn't put Chris on speaker, so I only heard Guy's end of the conversation.

"Hey, Chris, it's Guy... How are you, man?... I'm fine, thanks... Yeah, I'm actually at the restaurant right now... Yeah, it's pretty busy... Yeah, John's here... Dude, that sucks... Oh, the doctor said stay in bed?... Did he say a hospital bed?... No? Fantastic. I'll see you in fifteen minutes."

That's when I realized that sometimes business rules are democratic, while in other instances, you're looking at a totalitarian dictatorship. In this situation, it was the latter. If a guy like Guy tells you to get to work, you get to work, especially if it's early in your tenure with the company. From that day forward, for the entirety of my five-year run at Hooters, I never took a day off. I worked shifts in wheelchairs when I blew out my knee, I worked shifts on crutches, and I worked shifts when I had bronchitis. In retrospect, those were all terrible ideas, but I had a streak to uphold. I never called in sick, not once.

I could've taken the time off—I'd earned it, after all—but sometimes you have to understand that the people who make the rules—the Guys of the world—can write unwritten rules whenever they damn well please. And when you understand the unwritten rules, *follow them*, because doing so is a fantastic anti-Drift move.

(A quick digression from Drift-speak: The most notable unwritten Hooters rule was, "We're paying you to be here, so be here." Regarding illness, *my* unwritten rule at my company is, if you're sick, stay home, because A) For most office jobs, the vast majority of tasks can be done from bed. If somebody's sick and they know stuff has to get done, they're still going to get it done whether it's sitting in my office or on their couch, in their pajamas. And B) I'm a germophobe. It's been said that the magic is in the hallways—things pop more when your team can meet face-to-face—and I can't argue with that, but a hallway filled with coughs and sneezes isn't at all magical. If you own a company, it's not fair to expect your employees to come to an office when they feel like shit, because *they don't own the company*. For them to work harder and more efficiently, they have to love what they're doing, be fulfilled, like their colleagues, and, most importantly for the sake of this discussion, happily work when they don't feel like working. Anyhow, back to our regularly scheduled book.)

Now that I had a greater understanding of the unwritten Hooters rules, I wasn't fazed when the company's top brass sent me to messed-up shops in random parts of the country. After Melbourne, it was off to Oklahoma City. Then Atlanta. Then Orlando. Then Detroit. It got to the point that when I settled into my new apartment in another new city, I'd walk into a furniture store to buy a couch, and the first thing I'd do is pick it up to see how heavy it was. The weight of it mattered to me almost as much as how it looked; if it was heavy, no matter how attractive it was, my attitude was, *Screw that, I'm not buying this thing*, because I knew that at some point I'd have to lift it. (Another unwritten rule at Hooters: When they relocated you, they gave you a U-Haul. No professional movers, just a truck and the vague promise that some of the cooks from the restaurant might help you carry your shit up four flights of stairs.)

When the decision-makers relocated me, I dragged Dave Levins—my Hooters partner-in-crime who you met two chapters ago—almost everywhere I went. Soon after I'd been promoted to multi-unit management—which is upper management, one step below vice president—I was in Grand Rapids, Michigan, with Dave, who I promoted to general manager. Dave's family, however, was in Atlanta, and they were having some issues. The issues were so bad that he was considering a move back to Georgia to sort things out.

Coincidentally enough, I had to fly to the corporate offices in Atlanta for a big meeting with all the area guys, one of whom was named Todd Fetters. Todd was hired around the same time I was, but, unlike myself, he'd been based in one location for his entire Hooters tenure: Atlanta.

Soon after the meeting started, I piped up: "Guys, I have this problem. I've got Dave, and I hate to lose him. He's amazing. He's been my right-hand guy forever, but he's got some family issues, and I need to get him back to Atlanta, and we've got to find him an opening down here. We need to get him a position as a GM somewhere in the area."

Todd said, "I like all my GMs. I don't want to move any of my people."

"I get that," I said, "but you have to understand, this dude has done so much for the company. I've moved him, like, five times.

He's picked up his family and moved them, like, five times, just for Hooters. Now the company needs to do this for him."

Todd stared right at me and said, "Moving doesn't mean shit."

Seriously. He actually said, "Moving doesn't mean shit." Apparently the man thought he was a wolf of Wall Street.

I wanted to murder him. I wanted to absolutely jump across the table and rip his throat out, partly because it was a dick thing to say, but partly because, in that moment, I realized he was right. He'd climbed through the Hooters system with the exact same fluidity and speed that I had, but by simply telling the decision-makers, "I own a house here in Atlanta; I won't move." So he didn't have to move.

I then understood that the carrot of advancement that had been dangled in front of me since day one was, in some ways, bullshit. It's fair to assume that if you go the extra mile or ten—and willingly move from Oklahoma City to Atlanta to Orlando to Detroit—you should get promoted quicker than everybody else at your level. Not promoted at the same speed. Promoted *quicker*.

Thing is, that was just an assumption. There was nothing in the Hooters employee handbook that said, "Going from location to location—and kicking ass at each spot—will shoot you up the corporate ladder at the speed of sound." But when enough people in authority tell you that's how things work, you believe them. It was nothing more than a manipulation tactic to get me to go fill a hole where they needed me to go. (Luckily for Dave, there were multiple supervisors in the Atlanta area, one of whom was more than happy to make a space for him.)

You see, unwritten rules tend to come from people of authority, and if you hear and see something enough, you'll begin to believe it. That's a problem, because sometimes people who are telling you unwritten rules don't always have your best interests at heart. Figuring out the hows, whens, wheres, and whys of unwritten rules will keep your job-Drifting to a minimum.

This is something that was made evident to me during the beginning of my tenure on *The Apprentice*. My early performance on the show was fantastic, if I do say so myself. Right off the bat, I led the team to a win on several tasks, and we were rolling, but after a few weeks, my team hit a nasty losing skid, and the reason we kept losing was because we weren't playing properly. We weren't reading the rules thoroughly enough. We weren't understanding exactly what we were going to be judged on.

The show's hardest task—and possibly the hardest task on any reality contest show, ever—was called Motel Hell. In a nutshell, they took us to a shitbag hotel by the Jersey Shore and gave us thirty-six hours to restore four rooms and run the hotel.

When dividing up the workload, I told my team, "I'm going to oversee the renovation of the rooms. I'm going to get them 100 percent done." I then worked my ass off for thirty-six hours straight—no sleep, meals on the run, very little chance to go to the bathroom—and, sure enough, I got them done. False modesty aside, they looked great, *way* better than the other contestants' work. Don't believe me? Google it.

Despite our killer aesthetics, we lost. Why? Because we didn't fully absorb the rules. We were too focused on the renovations and having the best-looking end product, but man, were we off. The rules for the task clearly stated that we'd be judged on the customer comment cards and the quality of the rooms was just one small part; customer satisfaction was the most important criterion.

The other teams took that to heart and did little to renovate their rooms—they just made sure they had a pool party with their guests where they played guitar, and sang, and drank, and everybody had a great night. Yeah, their rooms were a little crappy—they didn't really care, because they just wanted to be on television—but there was only one line on the customer card about this, and that line didn't pose the question *How did your room look?* We devoted all our energy into what turned out to be a small aspect of the task. If we'd planned a party, we would have won.

All we needed to do was pay complete attention to the rules. Unfortunately, as demonstrated by another crappy *Apprentice* performance, we didn't learn our lesson right away.

This task in question involved painting giant graffiti on a wall in Harlem hyping the launch of a new *Gran Turismo* video game. From an artistic standpoint, my team's mural was spectacularly better than the other teams, but we weren't entering an art show, and we should've known that. Our beautiful mural artwork didn't have a lot to do with the video game, a bad idea when you're in an *advertising* contest. The other teams slapped together stuff that looked like it had been thrown up by some third graders, but the art was all about the video game, and that's all the client wanted.

The point burned itself in my mind when one of the video game execs came to judge our mural, and, after peering at it for a good two minutes, said, "This is beautiful, but it doesn't really have anything to do with us."

In effect, we won the wrong contest. By not understanding what we needed to accomplish—by putting our heads down and our blinders on, and without proper preparation—we ended up working against ourselves. (I should note that I didn't fully absorb this lesson until I watched the episodes. When you're in it, you're *in it*; you don't quite *get it*. Then when you see the other teams follow the rules to the letter, you think, *Shit, why didn't we do that?*)

During this stretch, back in the real world, my friend Dan was running a tech firm called Pattern Recognition. Dan had a ton of original ideas, but he didn't know how to execute the day-to-day operations, so he asked me to come on as both a partner and COO. We were thrilled with my spot on *The Apprentice*, because that sort of visibility would be nothing but helpful.

I should note that Pattern Recognition was financed by Dan's father, and the father's best friend. Keep that in mind.

When *The Apprentice* saw the light of day, I made the mistake of falling down the chat room rabbit hole. There was a website called Television Without Pity, the central hub for all things reality show. They had forums where thousands upon thousands of reality show obsessives could discuss the stars of *The Apprentice*, and *Survivor*, and *The Real Housewives of Wherever*.

When it came to me, Television Without Pity had plenty to discuss, because my trajectory on *The Apprentice* went straight up, then straight down. To this day, some fans believe I took the greatest nosedive in reality show history. After three episodes, if Vegas posted odds on that show, I'd have been, by far, the favorite. After four episodes, not so much.

At first, most of the comments about me were along the lines of, "He's the man!" But that was when I was doing well. After I got creamed in a few tasks and the editing kicked in, it became all vitriol, all the time. It was like I was an invisible man who walked into a cocktail party where I was the subject of every conversation, good and bad.

Unfortunately, I let America's visceral hatred of me get under my skin, and it screwed with my head. When shit like that gets into your psyche, it impacts everything in your life, including your performance at work.

I was in such a bad place I was screwing up left and right at Pattern Recognition, which was very unlike me. (You'd think that after being on a reality show about business, I'd be good at business forever. You'd be wrong.) It got to a point where Dan began interviewing potential replacements for me, and I couldn't blame him one bit. I let him down, and I'm not ashamed to say it.

But at the time, I was oblivious to what Dan was up to. We went down to New Orleans for a wedding along with most of the company. Afterward, I came home to return to work, but Dan stayed down there. That was odd.

I learned about the "replace John" meetings when I found out that Dan was staying at an expensive hotel and running up massive charges on the corporate credit card, just the kind of information that COOs always find out about. So I called the partners—who, if you'll recall from a few paragraphs back, were Dan's father and the father's BFF—and asked them, "How irresponsible is Dan acting?"

Naturally, they didn't respond with any kind of support because there was no world in which they were ever going to side with me over Dan…and I didn't realize that.

I ignored an important rule for avoiding The Drift: Know when you're beat.

I actually tried to get my partner's dad to side with me—a Drift move, for sure. Not only had I let my mind mess up my buyout from the company, but it also cost me my friendship with an awesome guy.

Listen, Drifting can take many forms—apathy, complacency, depression—but desperation always seems to push your decision-making in the worst direction. Remember that the next time the chips are really stacked against you: Slow down and think about the rules. I completely overestimated my worth to the company and ignored the unwritten rules. I didn't play the game.

This applies to relationships of all sorts, romantic ones included. (No, this isn't a love advice book, but stick with me here for a second.) We've all had relationships where, due to your shitty behavior, you got dumped, after which you wound up being completely embarrassed by said behavior. If you can admit to yourself—and your former better half—that you were a bad partner, then you can take the loss, absorb the lessons, and move on. That, right there, is a logical rule.

Despite the fact that I'd been on one of the most popular television shows in the country, and despite the fact that I'd salvaged goodness-knows-how-many Hooters locations, and despite the fact that I ran one of the most successful nightclubs in the country, this Pattern Recognition mess sent me Drifting. Think about it: I was fired by Donald Trump, hundreds of thousands of reality show fans thought I was an asshole, and I lost a job with a company created by a close friend. I could've closed the shades, curled up in bed, and let life happen to me.

But I didn't. I put on my helmet and kept moving forward. Back in the day, I got far too familiar with The Drift, and it sucked, but one thing I knew for damn sure is that it wouldn't happen again, in part because I learned that some rules are written, and some are unwritten, and some are made up as you go along, and some are straight-up ridiculous. But regardless of what sort of rules you're dealing with, make them work for you.

Win that Monopoly game.

Get an A on your school paper.

Paint the right mural.

And use a damn pen.

CHAPTER 5

SEE DIFFERENT

WORKING THE ANGLES . . . BUT IN A NICE WAY

In 2004, a racehorse named Smarty Jones won the Kentucky Derby and the Preakness Stakes; if he took the Belmont Stakes, he'd become the first horse to win the Triple Crown since Affirmed way back in 1978. That was a massive deal, something that even those who were ambivalent about horse racing understood.

Which begs the question, "Is Gafford ambivalent about horse racing?"

Pretty much. But I'm not ambivalent about ideas. Clever ideas. Original ideas. Ideas that lead to other ideas. Ideas that lead one out of The Drift. To that end, let's talk about Brian McDowell.

A super-loud, super-brash guy from New Jersey, McDowell was about 5'6", kind of chunky, and more than a little pugnacious, the kind of person who'd stroll into a bar where everybody was drinking whiskey and yell, "*You guys got a piña colada?!*"

Brian was one of my castmates on *The Apprentice,* where he gained notoriety as the only guy who *asked* Donald Trump to fire him, a wish that Trump granted on episode number two.

As is the case with everybody who gets whacked on the show, Brian wasn't literally sent home, but rather put up in a huge apartment that was affectionately known as "The Flop." Now you don't actually flop in The Flop; rather, the producers give you a list of fun things to do around New York City, all on their dime. When we Floppers weren't enjoying the city, we hung out with the other contestants whom Trump had dispatched, giving us the opportunity to bond with a vast array of businesspeople, which arguably turned out to be the most important aspect of the experience.

One day at The Flop, Brian told us, "I've gotta go watch the Belmont. I *have* to!"

"You're a horse racing fan?" I asked.

"*I! Have! To! Watch! The! Belmont!*" As usual, Brian was loud.

I said, "All right, fine, relax. We'll find a sports bar. We'll go watch this horse race."

On the way to the bar, Brian could barely stay still. "This is gonna be great! I can't wait!"

I asked, "So you like the ponies?"

He said, "Not really. But I bought a thousand two-dollar win tickets for Smarty Jones for the Derby, and another thousand for the Preakness, then another for the Belmont."

Ah, there was money on the line. Now his excitement and jitteriness made sense. "Cool," I said. "Let's go watch this race."

We indeed watched the race, where Smarty Jones was upset by a horse named Birdstone, who came into the Belmont with odds of 36–1. Brian was furious. I tried to calm him down as he cursed and pounded the table. "Bro," I said, "you already won two races. At the very least, you broke even, right?"

He said, "That's not what it was about. I was going to take all my win tickets for all three races and license a picture of the horse and turn it into a collectible print and sell them on QVC for $1,000 each. Nobody's won a Triple Crown in forever, and horse people would buy this thing, guaranteed, and I'd make thousands and thousands of dollars on a $6,000 investment."

My jaw hit the floor. I mean, here's this Jersey guy who doesn't give a shit about horse racing, but he found a plausible, original way to profit from a major sports and cultural event, strictly because he looked for an angle—and found one that nobody else saw.

Hmm. The big takeaway there—aside from learning that if you wanted to enjoy a chill night at a bar, don't go with Brian McDowell—was that it's easy to find an angle, but it's hard to find an *original* angle, so you have to work the angles until they work for you.

Some consider the phrase "working the angles" to have a negative connotation, and I get that—it might make you think of George Clooney and Brad Pitt in *Ocean's Eleven*, huddled up in a hotel room, scheming to take down Andy Garcia. The fact is, it's more about finding a path that nobody's gone down, finding a route that nobody's taken, finding a rule that you can exploit. I haven't done a study, but I suspect that if you look at every single person who succeeds in life—every single person who's managed to avoid or escape The Drift—it's because they either did something that nobody's ever done before or they took a proven concept and improved on it in a way that nobody thought they could.

Let's talk about JJ Todd, a travel hacking expert and my personal travel concierge.

JJ not only books all my travel, but he advises me on how to get the most out of my credit card miles. No one is better at working the system than JJ. Don't believe me? Well, check out this story, originally heard on my podcast, *Escaping the Drift*.

> In a world where savvy tactics meet the mundane routine of daily commuting, JJ found himself in a bind when his car's transmission failed. Faced with a week-long repair, JJ opted to rent a car. But instead of a straightforward rental, he devised a clever angle to maximize reward points.
>
> JJ realized that he passed a rental facility every day on his way to work. Why not rent a different car each day and accumulate points? He discovered that each rental earned him between 600 and 1,200 points. So, he embarked on a unique journey, renting a new car daily, rotating through models like the Ford Fiesta and Chevy Spark, each experience adding to his growing collection of points and stories.
>
> JJ's strategy didn't stop there. He enjoyed this process so much that, upon getting his car back, he sold it and committed to renting full-time. He negotiated a set rate with the rental company, ensuring his costs remained low. Over five years, JJ rented over two hundred cars annually, reaping benefits beyond the points: no registration fees, no maintenance costs, and often, free gas.
>
> But JJ's adventurous spirit didn't settle there. In 2017, he received an email offer from Hertz: 5,250 United miles for every rental. Doing the math, he realized the potential for immense value. Starting with single rentals and escalating to renting multiple cars in a day, Jake meticulously played by the rules to maximize his gains.

> Finally he asked the GM, "Can I just rent cars and not take them?" The GM, seeing his profits go up and costs stay down, agreed.
>
> He befriended Peter, a rental agency employee, and together they tested the system's limits. They discovered they could process up to fifty rentals in a day before the system buckled. By the end of the promotion, JJ had earned over 3.4 million miles, equating to approximately $120,000 in flight value, all for an outlay of around $12,000.
>
> In an unexpected twist, Hertz celebrated JJ's exploits. When he hit his millionth mile, they threw him a party, complete with balloons and a congratulatory cake. All of this happened simply because he opened his eyes and mind to the possibilities around him.

If you look with wide eyes and an open mind, you can find angles everywhere, even in arenas that seem utterly angle-free.

Like big pharma.

My sister, as I've mentioned, is just about the smartest of the Gafford clan, so when she offers up a business suggestion, I'll generally roll with it. In 2000, she was hired for a consulting gig with an insurance agency in Texas. Soon after she began her evaluation of the company, she called me up and said, "You and me, we're opening an insurance agency."

I said, "Ummmm, we are?"

"Yeah. These people have the best angle I've ever seen."

If my sister says it's the best angle she's ever seen, you can be sure it's an amazing angle.

You can't become a licensed insurance agent without, logically enough, getting a license, which, in Florida, means taking a forty-hour course. (At least that's how long you are supposed to spend on it.) I managed to get through the entire course in a day with a passing grade, and, a week after my sister recruited me, I was official, at which point I learned the ins and outs of what made this Texas agency so special.

This company specialized in Medicare supplements, and I found out that, with Medicare, there's Part A coverage and Part B coverage. This was before Part D—drug coverage—was added to the equation, so patients could use only A and B, then get a Medicare supplement to fill in the gaps where their policy was lacking. Most people buy a Medicare supplement right when they turn sixty-five, and then it's locked into that price for their lifetime, and they never change it because it's too expensive. But they were on their own when it came to buying their prescriptions.

So the angle here was a little known and never acknowledged handshake agreement between the US government and all the drug companies, that agreement being, *As long as you provide medicine for free to seniors who don't meet certain income requirements, we won't hassle you about your drug pricing.* This worked out for the drug companies, mostly because they never told the people who were buying their pills about the agreement.

But this particular Texas insurance agency, after they did their research, became experts at getting people free medicine.

Yes. That's right. Free medicine. Here's how it worked.

Let's say the patient in question was paying $150 a month for the Medicare supplement policy, on top of the $600 they shelled out for their meds. The insurance agency, using the angles they found in their research, learned that they could manipulate the system so the patient had to pay $200 for their monthly insurance premium, but $0 for their prescriptions. A life-changing savings for the client and an easy sale for the agency.

We took that paradigm to Florida, and it was like shooting fish in a barrel. Every appointment I had, I closed. The downside was that there was no excitement to it. Going from running a nightclub to sitting in elderly people's living rooms and discussing their health was a big change, to say the least...but man, did it print money. And without the angle, it wouldn't have succeeded.

In real estate, we often deal with people who may not have the credit or the down payment to achieve their housing dreams—and I get that. I demolished my credit at one point in my life like there was prize money for doing so, and considering what you now know about my professional path, are you surprised? I remember walking into a bank, hoping they would open an account for me, and when I was rejected, well, the feeling of shame was indescribable.

I never want anybody to feel that way. It's brutal.

That all being the case, I make it a point to treat somebody who can't qualify for a loan with the utmost respect. You don't know why their credit isn't up to snuff—it might be due to a family tragedy, or debt due to crappy health insurance, or simply a lack of financial know-how. Regardless of how the person in question got to this point, they're well aware they are at that point, and they know their credit is trash. They know they didn't pay their bills on time.

They feel terrible. So I approach it from a different angle and choose to give them something the financial world won't at that moment: dignity and respect.

I train my people to know that whenever they find themselves speaking with a potential homebuyer who's trying to dig themselves out of their financial mess, they should always look across the table and say, "Look, here's the deal: If this is really a dream of yours—if owning a home is *really* a dream that you want to achieve—I'm going to help you get there. I'm going to connect you with good credit repair people. We're going to get started on the road to this. I don't care if it takes two months or two years, I'm going to be here to help you get this done. We'll do it together."

Soothing, right? A great way to lead them out of The Drift—sometimes all it takes is someone to believe in you. But I also have to look out for my business, so here's what they'll say next: "While we're working on this, if you know anybody else who might want to buy or sell a house, please refer them to me."

That may seem cheesy, asking somebody for a referral when they're dealing with one of the most complex problems they'll ever face, but I think it's a sign of respect. Too many people are made to feel like shit—sometimes by a banker, or a Realtor, or a landlord, or a debt collector—if their credit is messy. If you make them feel like it's okay—if they believe they've been heard and understood—they will love you. This approach has helped me create what I like to call an army of referral goodwill.

The thing is, all money issues are not created equal. Sometimes a messed-up financial portfolio is simply due to overspending, and it's difficult, if not impossible, to find an angle to fix it and move forward. But new eras bring new issues, and new issues require new angles.

So let's talk crypto.

There's a group of kids here in Vegas—I call them kids even though they're between twenty and thirty years old—who I refer to as the Crypto Mafia. They figure out every opportunity to exploit any system to make money, in part because they're so connected, and so fast at gathering information. They've demonstrated to me that if you want to think differently, one of the easiest ways to do so is to see how other people are thinking differently, and a lesson I've learned from the Crypto Mafia is to pay attention to what's happening in the world on Discord and Telegram.

By staying plugged in, the Mafia was trading in front of the herd. They'd pop into those chat rooms, and seem to be ahead of when everyone else was going to dump, say, Dogecoin, always ending up on the right side of trades. I'm not an expert in this by any means, but I have a hunch that if they were doing this with stocks, it may be an issue, but it's crypto, which is deregulated currency, so, as far as I know, this is all good.

These kids, they always figure out what's next. When Amazon stores became prevalent, they jumped onto that train and charged business and individual entrepreneurs, say, $30,000, to build up their store and do their fulfillment... and they sold a gazillion of those packages. (Note, this business did wind up with a bunch of copycats who used the same paradigm but were scamming customers.) To their credit, they didn't just go out to clubs and blow the money, but rather they bought luxury cars and started a fleet of high-end rentals. An angle leading to an angle leading to an angle. If you were a horse racing fan—which, as noted, I'm not—you might call that the Angle Trifecta.

These kids often find angles in the oddest places, one of those odd places being the United States government. For instance, employee retention credit, or ERC. ERC is free government cash money for companies that didn't lay people off during the COVID lockdown. To take advantage, all companies need to do is spend ten minutes filling out a piece of paperwork.

Ten. Minutes.

For my ten minutes, I received approximately $700,000. And before you scoff and/or roll your eyes, it's worth noting that throughout the pandemic, I treated my employees like gold.

These Crypto Mafioso count on the fact that most people don't understand simple things, and they use that to their advantage. These guys file ERCs for people who don't know how to do so, and in return, they'll take a 20 percent cut.

If I hired them to take care of this ten-minute task for me, they would have earned $140,000, which shakes out to an hourly rate of $840,000, and a yearly salary of $1,747,200,000.

The thing I love about this group of kids is they're always on the pivot, *always*. They never get complacent. They're always looking for the next thing, and they inevitably find it because they stay connected, they share information, and they push it forward. And if you come across anybody like that, keep them in your life, because you need to be around people who are constantly looking for angles. Spend enough time with them, and their approach to business and life will rub off on you.

One of the biggest differences in my life from when I was Drifting to where I am now is the quality of conversations I have with other people. In my previous, struggling life, the conversations I would have were, at best, frivolous and, at worst, talking about other people. I can't stress this enough, but gossiping about other people is one of the biggest currents that can keep you Drifting. Instead, seek to have conversations about ideas, concepts, and success. Watch your conversations change, watch your life change.

Which brings me to mastermind groups.

Some feel that mastermind groups are fantastic places to mix and mingle with experts in angle playing. Which might have you wondering, *What the hell is a mastermind group?* Here's how Tony Robbins explained it: "A mastermind group is a group of peers who meet to give each other advice and support. It's similar to mentoring, but has several important differences. First, it will have five or six members, instead of being a one-on-one meeting. In a mastermind group, you will both give and receive advice, while in a mentorship, you'll typically be on the receiving end. Mastermind groups can also involve brainstorming, educational presentations, and even discussing personal issues. Many people think of these groups as mastermind classes, but they are not a class. There is no single teacher with a prepared lesson. So what is a mastermind group really? It is a 'meeting of the minds'—a place where you can speak the truth and expect it in return."

Based on that explanation, it seems like a mastermind group is the be-all and end-all of networking, a place where you can learn everything about angles, and crypto, and ERCs, and how to get free medicine.

I'm a member of several high-level masterminds, and they range from very organized organizations like "Boardroom Mastermind"—a group that has quarterly meetings across the country—to simple text groups that I have on my phone with awesome names like "Dicks and Deals." The point is, no matter where you are on your journey, there's no reason not to start connecting today with like-minded individuals who can help shorten your time frame to success. It's up to you to find them.

But you know what? You only get out of something what you put into it, and in my mastermind group experience, not everybody goes the extra inch, let alone the extra mile. If a group isn't providing you the same value you are putting in, find a new one, start a new one, but don't keep Drifting.

In other words, part of learning how to play the angles is learning where you shouldn't play the angles... which, if you think about it, is an angle unto itself.

Looking for an edge in a nontraditional manner is far from a guaranteed win—if an angle leads to a guaranteed win, it would be traditional, and would cease to be an angle. But if you do it right—if you pick the right horse, or the right insurance plan, or the right cryptocurrency—you can start bidding farewell to The Drift.

CHAPTER 6

SELL THIS

MAKE THE WORLD WORK FOR YOU

Using myself as an example, one way to avoid The Drift, if not escape it entirely, is to learn how to sell. It doesn't matter *what* you decide to sell; it's just key that you decide to sell *something*.

I'm dead serious. And don't roll your eyes. I know a lot of people hear the word *sales*, and they immediately think of the guy in the loud plaid jacket standing on a used car lot, the guy who asks, "What do I have to do to get you into a Toyota today?" (Admittedly, as someone that learned to sell on a car lot, I've used an iteration of that line. But sometimes it works!) The truth about sales is you're selling every day, whether you want to admit it or not.

You're selling yourself to the person you're chatting up at the bar who you want to date.

You're selling a future to your kids when you tell them to do their homework and go to bed on time.

You're selling sage advice and decades of wisdom when you write about The Drift.

Whether or not you make sales a career, understanding some basics of selling is crucial. A great place to start that journey is by embracing public speaking.

You see, being a great salesman is being a great storyteller; the ability to tell stories succinctly and colorfully—and to inspire people in the process—is a skill that can take you almost anywhere. Now some people are born with it. Others develop it. And others have to develop what they're born with.

That last one is me. I had it. I just had to make it *better*.

When I was in eighth grade, I realized that on "Club Day" it was better to be in a club meeting than in class, so it was important to join as many clubs as I could, which is why I became a member of Future Farmers of America, a club that you might recall from the film *Napoleon Dynamite*.

It wasn't just about winning blue ribbons with the local cows—they somewhat oddly also had extemporaneous public speaking competitions. I was a decent talker, so I was selected to be on the team, and man, it wasn't as easy as you might think. It was really a trial by fire.

We'd be given a topic, then we'd have a whopping fifteen minutes to write a speech, after which we had to deliver it *immediately*. No time for a second draft, no time to rehearse, no time to grab a snack—just get up in front of the judges and discuss a random topic like how Florida Farm Bureau subsidies positively affect farmers in Florida. And keep in mind, *this was before the Internet*.

Despite being a middle schooler competing against high school kids, I would have won the title of Florida's Future Farmers of America State Extemporaneous Public Speaking Champion if it weren't for a much-disputed timekeeping issue. As I write this, I'm realizing it all sounds a tad silly—I mean, a farmers club that offers you the opportunity to lecture, and me complaining about the fact that I'm still adamant the judges can't operate a stopwatch. But sometimes the silliest situations offer you the greatest lessons.

I didn't know a whole lot about the Florida Farm Bureau. I didn't know a lot about subsidies. Honestly, I didn't know a whole lot about anything, but thanks to being born with the gift of gab, I could muddle my way through a speech, and even make it compelling.

How? By simply reading the room.

This is one of the keys to being a great communicator. It doesn't matter if you're standing in front of a room full of people delivering a speech or talking one-on-one to somebody you just met, you have to think big picture. Clumsy people focus on what they're going to say next, while in-tune people focus on how what they just said affected the people to whom they're speaking.

Focusing on the reaction of your audience will tell you if what you're saying is captivating or on the right track. But like they say, you can't win 'em all, and part of the art of being a great storyteller is knowing when you've lost the audience. It happens to the best of us, and when it happens, wrap it up and redirect the conversation.

If you think back, I guarantee you can come up with one instance of somebody you know that drones on about nothing, and you sit there with a glazed look, staring at them, repeating the same phrase over and over: "Wow, that's craaaaazzzzzy."

It's always, "Wow, that's craaaaazzzzzy."

When you say this, the person is failing, and now that you know when someone says this to you to take it as a cue, you won't fail.

But relying solely on the gift of gab isn't sufficient, because in order to craft a good narrative, you have to move people at a personal level, a gut level, and one way to do just that is via empathy. If you can weave a sincere sense of empathy into your selling and storytelling, you ramp up your chance to put an end to your Drifting.

For me, empathy is the ability to put yourself in other people's shoes. Sure, I got my PhD in selling cars, but back then, I never put myself in a customer's shoes. At that point in my life, I was all about *winning*, all about negotiating the best deal *for* the company *on behalf* of the company, and getting my bosses what they wanted.

But it was never empathetic selling.

I didn't ask the customer, "How big is your family? How much driving do you do each day, week, or month? What's your exact budget? What can I do to improve your car-buying experience?" Nor did I offer them a slice of my life, maybe tell them about the first time I bought a car, or commiserate with them about how difficult and frustrating the process can be.

When I first learned to sell, it was all about using tactics to do what I wanted the customer to do, which, of course, was to buy whatever I was selling. This runs the gamut from simple impulse buys (like Hooters T-shirts) to difficult buys (for example, cars), but when you get a little more complex sales cycle, you learn quickly you are not selling products—you're selling *solutions*.

By focusing on the customers' needs, and by understanding through empathy what problems they have and how your product can help solve those problems, you'll stop selling *people* and start achieving sales through *helping* people.

It's also helpful to believe in the product you're selling. And if you don't embrace the item 100 percent—if you think, *This product is fine, but it's not what I'd buy*—look for something in said item that gets you jazzed. Maybe you don't love the way the car drives, but you know that it gets great mileage in the city, so push that. Customers are generally more sophisticated than you might imagine, and most can sense when you're bullshitting them.

You can be a good salesperson without lying.

No, let me amend that: You can be a *great* salesperson without lying.

Once you're comfortable with your selling chops, it's time to get a sales job. Thing is, before you dive into that particular pool, you need to figure out how you want to get paid. You can find a position that offers a great salary but little or no commission, or you can interview for a gig that offers a tiny salary and a huge commission. Which should you take? Well, it's all based on personal preference. Some like the comfort of knowing what will be direct deposited into their bank account every other Friday, while others like to fly without a net, to bet on themselves, to take the chance that their numbers will exceed the company's expectations.

There's no correct or easy answer for this one—it's all about your level of risk aversion. But sometimes, in order to get out of The Drift, taking the risk on a commission-based life is the move. After all, betting on yourself could not only give you a higher earning ceiling, but it can also empower you to change your entire life. Me, I've hired people who, up to that point, had never earned more than $50,000 a year, but I've thrown them into that aforementioned commission-based life, and, in some cases, they'll pull in $300,000. All because they bet on themselves.

To that end, let's talk about Amber Anderson.

I don't hire fully inexperienced people. If you want to work for me, you need to go cut your teeth and learn the basics of what you're doing somewhere else. What with parenting, husband-ing, and running a growing business, I don't have the bandwidth to teach anybody the ins and outs of real estate. Once you demonstrate you have some chops, you can come aboard.

But there are exceptions.

One afternoon, Amber Anderson came into my office, parked herself in the lobby, then, when she saw me, chased me down and told me that she was a brand-new agent and she wanted to work for me. Once I heard the words *brand* and *new*, I told her that I appreciated her interest, but she should come back when she had a few sales under her belt.

She said thank you and headed out.

But she came back the next day.

And the next.

And the next.

That's tenacity. I can explain real estate to you, but tenacity, serious tenacity, *legitimate* tenacity can't be taught. You either have it, or you don't.

Amber had it. And I hired her. And she quickly went from lobby stalker to top producer on my team.

All that said, tenacity can only get you so far. There are a number of foundational concepts that will facilitate your sales journey.

First: Sales equals control.

You have to maintain control of the client in all situations, because if *they* take control, it's over. You lose control, you lose the sale, or you make the sale at a lesser number, neither of which is a desired outcome.

I learned this lesson early in my car-selling career. Check out this control experiment on human nature I picked up at the car dealership:

- Walk up to a car-hunting customer.
- Ask a couple of questions.
- When you get an idea of what kind of car they're in search of, say, "Follow me," then turn your back and walk toward the dealership without turning around.

Like clockwork, I could walk one hundred yards to the door of the dealership, open the door, and, sure enough, they'd be standing right there. But if you ever turned around mid-journey, they'd likely stop and say, "We're just looking."

It's not about getting the client to do what you want—in most cases, it's just that you have a better understanding of how the process should go, and if the client will let you guide them through the sale, it's always a better experience than them trying to force their way through it.

Second: Set expectations.

Every quality sales process should have an objective, no exceptions.

Almost every week, an agent will tell me, "John, I'm exhausted. These clients run me ragged. They call me at all hours. They do this, they do that, blah blah blah." (Generally, my initial thought is, *You have clients, and in this climate, having clients isn't always a thing, so quit bitching.*) In order to keep the client happy—and keep me from bitching to other people in my industry—I teach my agents to deliver my client an expectation sheet, which includes stuff like ground rules for how long they have to call them back. (Is it twenty-four hours? Eight hours? Six hours? One hour? Ten minutes?)

Simply ask your clients what's acceptable to them on *every* type of communication, because if they happen to call and I don't get back to them right away, they know I'll reach out within the agreed-upon time frame. If they complain, I'll tell them to refer back to that sheet, which usually quashes the bad feelings before they can even start. It also establishes the fact that, even though I let them set the time frames, I'm maintaining the control by making sure their expectations stay within their initial parameters.

Third: Make it impossible to be misunderstood.

When I discuss a deal point with a potential client, I'll shoot them an email with the details that were just discussed in order to avoid a you-said-this-no-I-said-that situation. When it gets into a you-said-I-said deal, all semblance of control can fly out the window. If there is any ambiguity in a conversation where your client feels like you were lying about something you'd previously discussed, you're going to lose something worse than control, which is trust. This technique will always protect you from having to argue with your clients about something that was said because, remember, the prize for winning an argument with a client is losing a client.

The people who allow you to do your job in sales always have the best experience and get the best deal. The people who want to do it their way often have a terrible experience and normally get the worst deal. And this doesn't just apply to real estate and cars, but any transaction when there's negotiation involved.

The most important thing to understanding any sales process is that you can't sell something to somebody at a time they don't need it. More importantly, you may only be able to sell something to someone in the moment when they do, because timing is everything.

Take the case of entrepreneur Irina Wynn, who told her story on my podcast.

Frustrated with airline delays in Europe, she quickly learned that airlines in Europe, unlike America, have a financial penalty when the plane is late to the gate or the airline loses your luggage.

Most people just don't take the time to file the claims, and she saw opportunity in this. Her company will earn a net profit of $15 million this year filing claims on behalf of delayed passengers. The key to her success is she understands her staff has got to take advantage of timing. Most people won't go to the trouble of filling out forms or following up on the website to file a claim after they've left the airport.

So her staff works timing to the max. She has crews of salespeople waiting in the area—several airports across Europe—and as soon as they learn of a delayed flight, six of her associates rush to the gate to catch people at the height of their frustration, at which point they'll be more likely to hire her company to file their claims. This is an elite understanding of sales timing as well as process.

Every sale has a process that is designed to get the client from point A to point Z with as little friction as possible; and notice I said with as little friction, and not as fast as possible. There are steps to the sales process, and every step has a goal. Skipping ahead and not staying focused on the individual goal of where you are in the sales process will cause confusion to the client and friction to the sale. The moral of this story is, don't let your newfound knowledge cause you to skip steps or give away profit. Work your system like it's your first day.

In a certain sense, all of this sales stuff—the control stuff, the consistency stuff, the storytelling—boils down to process and communication.

Let's pick one entity that combines both process and communication. We'll roll with voicemail.

When you leave a voicemail, you must stay true to the only goal of that voicemail—to get them to call you back—that's it. Look at it this way: No answering machine in the history of answering machines has ever bought anything, so why are you pitching to it? For example, if you're contacting somebody to whom you want to sell a bunch of widgets, don't leave a voicemail like, "Hey there, this is This Guy from This Guy's Widgets. Just calling to see if I can sell you some widgets."

There are two consequences of that message:

1. You just tried to sell a widget to an inanimate object that's never going to buy anything from you.
2. The human who owns the voicemail recorder now has all the information they need to decide *not* to call you back.

On the other hand, if your message goes, "Hey, it's This Guy. I have too much information to leave on a voicemail, so call me back," your potential contact might well think, *Who's This Guy? He sounds like I know him. What's too long to leave on a voicemail?* No specificity in the voicemail equals curiosity, and that might just get you a callback.

Let me explain it like this. Did you almost die today? You're probably thinking, *Um, no,* but I beg to differ. If you got into a car and drove around for a couple of hours, there's a good chance that there were hundreds of other people in 4,000-pound death machines coming straight at you a few feet away. They passed by like they do every other time, and it never occurred to you how easy it would have been for the other drivers to swerve into your lane and kill you.

Why is that?

Well, as human beings, we are hardwired to live a fight-or-flight existence. This programming served us well in ancient times, keeping us from getting eaten by large animals. But today, our brains compartmentalize things they deem not to be a threat, which allows us to travel in our cars without screaming every time we pass another driver.

Your brain also compartmentalizes things that happen in everyday life, often looking for patterns to make your decision-making easier. At a clothing store, for example, when you see a salesclerk coming toward you, before they can even open their mouth, you've raised your hand to say you're just looking. You've programmed yourself to do this.

Believe me, as soon as anyone hears the phrase "How are you doing today?" their brain will immediately think, *Telemarketer*, and you're done before you start, so when starting a sales call, use any other greeting in the world.

As noted, all good salespeople have a process, and the most important part of that process is staying within the goals of each step. For example, when my team gets a potential client on the phone, the point of the call isn't to sell them a house, but rather to get them into the office. Everything they're doing is geared toward closing an appointment—*everything*.

Many Realtors will hear a client tell them on the phone, "I want to buy a three-bedroom, two-bathroom house in Green Valley with a pool, and my budget is $300,000." The Realtor will then proceed to spend the next ten minutes telling them why that's not reasonable or feasible.

My team, on the other hand, will say, "Great, come on down! When can you be at the office?" They'll then explain to the client how we can help them buy a home.

This is important not only because face-to-face interactions have more substance, but also if I'm going to crush somebody's dreams, I'm going to do it in person, because that gives me the opportunity to explain *why* their dream is unrealistic rather than be the faceless voice on the phone who says, "No."

As a salesperson, it's vital to remember that *you can't take shortcuts*. If you want to lose your sales mojo, go ahead and stop focusing on every little step of the process...as well as the *goal* of every little step of the process. You can't skip to the end. Don't handle steps A through D, then blow off E through Y, just so you can get to Z. If you have no idea what your process is, you won't know you're skipping steps, You will, however, "feel" the friction that's created by doing so, and thus they may not go for the deal at hand...or, worse, they may not work with you at all.

In terms of presentation, you're allowed to hype your product, but you're not allowed to lie. To that end, I hate it when agents make blanket statements like, "It's a great time to buy a house. Inventory is up, and I'm confident that interest rates are heading in the right direction." Maybe they're bullshitting, maybe they sincerely believe what they're putting out there, but regardless, sometimes it's *not* a great time for that specific client to buy a house, while for other clients, it's the perfect moment.

If you're making blanket statements like *This is good* or *This is bad*, you're losing, whether you know it or not, mostly because not all of us share a blanket. Maybe a potential client is dealing with a major life event, like they've had to take a job that earns them less than their previous position, or they're making the move from renting to buying. If you tell them, *Now is the time*, they might feel pressured or cornered, and there are a zillion Realtors out there, so if they're not comfortable with your approach—if they smell the bullshit—they'll ghost you.

You also can't bullshit *yourself*. With every sale, you have to stop and ask, *Does this project align with my values?* If you're pushing something you don't believe in—especially if it has a sense of shadiness about it—you're toast.

To that end, one day my assistant called. "There's a guy in the lobby," she said, "and something's not right."

"Um, okay, what does that mean?" I asked.

"I can't put my finger on it. He's a little old man. Just come in as soon as you can."

As soon as I sat down with the gentleman, it became obvious that he was suffering from dementia.

It came out that he'd been living in a Budget Suites hotel, he had all his stuff in his car, and he had a chunk of money, and one of the agents at my company went to the next step and put him in contract to buy a house. Thing is, the gentleman clearly didn't have the wherewithal to be buying a property by himself, and for my agent to push him to do so was flat-out wrong. That was totally out of alignment with my moral compass—and, for that matter, our company's moral compass—so, after the gentleman left, I immediately canned the agent and canceled the contract.

But I couldn't let it go. After doing some research, I discovered that the gentleman had been in the Navy, so, with the assistance of my wife and some agents from my team, they got him enrolled in the VA, which got him medical benefits, which enabled him to afford a great doctor. We also got him moved into a senior living apartment. Three of my agents took him out to help him buy furniture. Finally, we made certain that all his bills were on autopay, so he was set, and man, that was a great outcome. (If I'm being honest, my wife ran point on the entire process. But I'll give myself a tiny bit of credit. Just a bit.)

If your moral compass is straight—which, hopefully it is, because a straight moral compass can aid your journey out of The Drift—sometimes it's in the best interest of the client to tell them *no*.

As a businessperson, *no* is something you hate to say to a client, which might have something to do with the fact that we have to hear that word so often from our potential clients, and a *no* can be so painful at times that it drives some people right out of the sales business. But what if I told you there was a way to insulate yourself from the pain of hearing a prospect say *no*?

If you're a salesperson, you're going to spend a whole lot of time on the phone, and having your cell stuck to your ear, and delivering the same spiel over and over again, will, at times, feel like a time suck. But if you run the numbers, your phone work can be quite lucrative.

You're going to hear the word *no* a lot more than you can hear the word *yes*, but you can't let that get to you. Stop focusing on the rewards of success, because if you stay grounded and bulletproof, that makes the success sweeter.

Enter, valuing the *NO*.

Let's pretend you're a real estate agent in the average market. Let's say that when you sell a house, you earn on average around $12,000. Let's say you have to make one hundred calls to get enough appointments to eventually sell one house. That means the one successful call equals $12,000 while the ninety-nine unsuccessful calls equal zero dollars. This is how most people with a fear of rejection look at things.

But what if we look through this with a different lens? What if we valued *every* call, regardless of the outcome? That's $12,000 divided by one hundred, which means, in effect, each call earned you $120.

If I told you I'd pay you $120 to ring up a stranger and talk to them for somewhere between two and twenty minutes, you'd jump at that. You might not enjoy the job, and that's completely understandable. You'll get told to piss off on a regular basis, especially if you call during dinner. You'll get plenty of hang-ups. You'll get people who will curse at you as they hang up. But every time you get told, "Pound sand," you pocket $120. Makes it roll off the shoulders a little easier, doesn't it?

Also remember that it's not you, *the person*, taking the abuse—it's you, *the stranger*. I know when I make calls they're not telling John Gafford, husband, father, and hard worker, to piss off—they're telling every salesperson who's ever harassed them to piss off. If you're sensitive, your ego will get damaged, but you have to take yourself out of the equation. Once you do so, those $120 phone calls will get a whole lot easier.

Over the years, I've come to realize hang-ups are the second-best result of a cold call... the best result, of course, being a path to a sale. The faster somebody blows you off, the faster you'll know that they're not interested. I'd much rather have the phone slammed down on me than chat with a person who doesn't care what I have to say but is too polite to shut down the call. I tell all my salespeople, if somebody truly doesn't give a shit about what you're saying, the best thing for everybody involved is to shut it down.

All the lessons I've learned in the sales space have bestowed upon me the ability to give you a superpower. Don't get too excited—I'm not going to teach you how to fly, or bend a steel girder, or melt a weapon with your mind. What I'm going to tell you is this:

Never try to move anybody to do anything in sales without using the word *because*.

Before you scoff, you need to know this isn't me talking out of my ass.

Have you ever noticed how people will do what you ask if you just give them a reason—any reason? Harvard psychologist Ellen Langer ran a famous experiment that proves this. It happened back in the late '70s when people still relied on copy machines the way we rely on smartphones today. Long lines were common. So Langer had her team go out and try to cut in line—but here's where it gets interesting.

They tested three different approaches. One group simply asked, "Can I use the copier?" Another added a generic explanation: "Can I use the copier because I need to make copies?" The last group got more specific: "Can I use the copier because I'm in a rush?"

Now, you'd think people would only let someone cut if the reason was solid. But here's what happened: The group that just asked? About 60 percent got the green light. But when they added any reason—even something obvious like "because I have to make copies"—compliance jumped to over 90 percent.

Why? Because our brains like shortcuts. When we hear the word *because* we assume a valid reason is coming, and we tend to go along with it—even if the reason is weak.

That's a real-world example of how much of life is run on autopilot. People aren't thinking critically in every moment. They're reacting based on mental habits and patterns. The trick? Learn to recognize it—in others and in yourself—and use that awareness to start living more deliberately.

BECAUSE. Two syllables that can change your life. Here's how and why:

- Become a good storyteller BECAUSE it's the key to selling anything.
- Bet on yourself BECAUSE it's the bet you have the most control over.
- Be tenacious BECAUSE tenacity won't be denied.
- Maintain control BECAUSE it will make your clients happier.
- Be impossible to be misunderstood BECAUSE the prize for winning an argument with a client is losing a client.
- Trust the process BECAUSE without it you will be forced to scramble.
- Leave good voicemails BECAUSE people will call you back.

- Don't ask prospects "How are you doing today" BECAUSE if they think you're an annoying telemarketer, you are.
- Keep your moral compass points straight BECAUSE no one deal is worth your reputation.
- Value the no BECAUSE it makes you bulletproof from rejection.
- Use BECAUSE, well, BECAUSE.

CHAPTER 7

PLANS, GOALS, HONESTY, AND WINS

THERE'S NO MAGIC IN YOUR COMFORT ZONE

I can't stop talking about The Drift because it's so prevalent in my world. I see too many people with too much potential Drifting with the current, floating on the breeze, and bobbing and weaving their way through random ebbs and flows of life. When I see this person, I want to take them by the shoulders, look them in the eye, and say, "You won't swim out of that current until you can decide for yourself where you want to go, and then develop a plan to get there. Without some semblance of a game plan, you're just gonna Drift along for the rest of your life."

But it's not polite (or, I suppose, legal) to grab a stranger by the shoulders. So I wrote a book about it.

In any event, as you know by now, seven chapters in, I'm the ideal guy to break down how to escape The Drift because I spent far too much of my young adult life Drifting with the current and the breeze and the random ebbs and flows of life. In the moment, that Drift sometimes felt pretty good—after all, everybody loves sleeping until noon each and every day—but the more I Drifted, the more I realized that if I didn't make moves, I'd still be an aimless young adult when I was fifty years old. That's why you have to get serious when you're young, before you even have the chance to Drift.

I'm proud to say that my wife and I are doing a decent job of directing our kids away from Drifting, in part because we go out of our way to instill in them the importance of having a *plan*. But sometimes the kids, like all of us, fall into what I'll call a Niche Drift, the kind of Drift that impacts only a small part of anyone's life.

My son, for example, wasn't happy with his social situation at school. He's resistant to change, and was clinging desperately to this friend group he's had since third grade. Over a period of months, it dawned on him that he didn't have anything to talk to them about.

He said, "I feel like I don't fit in."

Nodding, I said, "Buddy, you probably don't. And there's nothing wrong with that, because if you felt like the same kid you were in third grade, that would be a problem. The interests you had in third grade are different from the interests you have as a ninth grader... and that's the case with this group of friends. If nobody you hang out with loves to talk sports, you need to find some friends that love to talk sports. If nobody in your group likes rock music, then find kids that like rock music. They're out there. The problem is, you won't explore outside your own bubble because it's comfortable to stay with what you know. But there's no magic inside your comfort zone."

I told him to build a mental avatar of a great friend, to figure out what traits would be conducive to a quality relationship, to figure out what common interests are the most essential to an enjoyable hang, to figure out whether this aspirational friend creation of his is quiet, or loud, or funny, or serious, or energetic, or chill.

To figure out a plan.

As I'm writing this, my son is working on the friend situation.

As you're reading this, I can guarantee you that he has it figured out.

As is the case with any advice, it's all fine and good to talk the talk, but if you can't follow your own guidance—if you don't walk the walk—you're wasting your time, your energy, and your chance to blow off Drifting. I recognize that I don't always do what I say, that I don't always make and stick with a plan... but, man, I try. Most of the time, when I try, it works. For instance: the $50 Fit Club.

The $50 Fit Club isn't an exercise app, nor is it a reality show coming to NBC in October. No, the $50 Fit Club is my creation, previously only shared with eight of my friends. Now, I'll share it with you.

The deal was that for two months, my friends and I had to work out every single day, then share a video of our workout with everybody via a text chain. Because all of us are getting older, we didn't get crazy. Not every day was about pumping iron, nor should it have been. You could be taking a walk, or doing one hundred crunches, but as long as you were active, it counted.

Here's the kicker: Every day you didn't do something physical, you had to throw $50 into a pot. If you want to make an excuse about why you can't get your lazy ass out of bed and go jog, run, walk, lift, get on the treadmill, get on the bike, whatever it may be, then it's going to cost you.

We decided at the end of the two months, we'd all go out to dinner with the money. I know, it doesn't really make sense to punctuate a fitness competition with twenty-ounce steaks and multiple bottles of bourbon, but motivation is motivation.

It turned out to be very, very effective. This group was so competitive that there were only eight missed workouts over those two months, and our $400 pot wasn't big enough for a quality steak-and-whiskey outing. We ended up having burritos and beer, but that didn't matter, because each of us dropped between five and ten pounds, all because we made a plan.

I remember a similar story about a study involving two minor league baseball teams. Each organization—and I mean the entire organization, from the GM to the receptionists—was issued a challenge: Lose more collective weight than the other team. Here's the kicker: One franchise was singled out and each employee was asked to provide a current photo of themselves in the skimpiest bathing suit imaginable, and was then told, "If your team doesn't win the challenge, these Speedo pictures will be flashed on the Jumbotron in the middle of a game."

Who do you think took home the prize? Naturally, it was Team Speedo for the "W," because you will move faster *away* from pain than you will run quickly *toward* pleasure.

One of the most important takeaways from these health challenges is that they're *simple*. Regular exercise and a better diet are *easy*. I'm not saying changing your lifestyle is a snap—I'm saying that the goal itself is simple. It's not elaborate, it's not convoluted. It's just... *I want to get healthy*. It doesn't require a treatise, just commitment and, you guessed it, a plan.

If your goals and plans are simple, succinct, and pointed, you're more likely to succeed. For example, when I'm coaching a prospective agent, the first question I'll ask is, "What's your goal?"

Inevitably, the goal will be a number. "I want to make $250,000 a year."

I'll ask, "Why? What are you going to do with the money?"

If the answer is, "Dunno. Just seems like a good number," I know right then and there that the chances they'll make that kind of money are slim, because if you don't attach a goal and a plan to your dream, it's considerably less likely to come to fruition.

I'd much prefer to hear, "I want to make $250,000 because I want to own my own home, and I want to set aside $47,800 a year for my kid's college tuition." If you tell me that, I know there's a far better chance you'll wake up each morning and make sales calls even when you *really* don't want to wake up and make sales calls. I know that if you look at your kid and think, *I'm giving my child a better home and a good education,* you'll jump over the hump to make one more call, to stay one more hour.

I went through this when I decided to quit smoking. I didn't have a plan, or a goal attached, just a vague belief that eliminating cigarettes from my life would be a good thing.

My first salvo was to follow an edict of, *I'll only smoke when I drink.* That, of course, is a stupid edict. When you're trying to figure out your way on this planet and climb out of The Drift, there's a good chance that you enjoy drinking. So yeah, I enjoyed drinking. And I drank. Not a lot, but enough to realize that the smoke-only-when-you-drink plan still had me sucking down almost a pack a week. This went on for months, until I went back to smoking when I *wasn't* drinking. Epic fail.

And then I met the woman who would become my wife, a woman who, five minutes into our first conversation, told me, "I'm not going to date a smoker."

Right then and there, I knew I wanted her more than I wanted any cigarette. I didn't care about smoking's health risks. I didn't care that I couldn't exercise properly with diminished lung capacity. I didn't care that I felt like shit the morning after I smoked too much. But I did care about dating this woman, and that was enough to get me to quit.

Along those lines, the older I get, the easier it is to make these sorts of life changes, because I'm feeling my mortality. I'm looking at my body in the mirror and thinking, *I don't want to be broken down at seventy-five. I don't want to go sliding into the grave without any tread left on the tires. I want to be there for my wife and kids. I want to fulfill all my business dreams. So I'm going to eat well, exercise well, sleep well, and have a positive mental attitude.*

This is why I drink hydrogen water, I sit on PMF mats, I do EWOT training, I meditate twice a day, and I take enough supplements to choke a goat. All of this would've seemed crazy to me before I had my family.

Family is probably the best motivator. If there's a partner and offspring in the equation, it makes it that much easier—and, frankly, more fun—to make and keep goals and plans. But you can't wait for the last minute to adjust your mindset: You need to get out of The Drift before you procreate, because your aimlessness isn't fair to the children; when you have kids, *you live for them.* If you're a Drifting parent, you might believe, *I've still got to be me and do what I want to do.*

Bullshit, bullshit, bullshit. I don't make any decisions at all without thinking about my kids.

When you're making plans and setting goals, honesty plays a huge role, whether that's being honest with your family, your friends, or your doctor. But the most important person with whom you need to be honest is yourself. I learned about that whole honesty-with-yourself thing during my tenure in the service industry.

If you're managing a restaurant or a bar, sure, you're the boss, but you still have a boss of your own, the boss who chooses the venue's opening and closing times, the boss who makes sure his employees are showing up at seven in the morning to prep for the lunch hour and the dinner rush. If you're the guy who owns the building, you have to be there to open the door.

But even if you're the owner, you still have a boss. And that boss is the time clock. And that is one unforgiving, immovable supervisor.

The first job I landed where I didn't have a time clock in any capacity was when I was promoted to an area supervisor position at Hooters. I was relocated to Michigan to oversee the state's stores, and it was the first time in my professional life that literally nobody knew where I was. I had no schedule. Nobody lorded over me. I was allowed the freedom to come and go as I pleased.

It was a disaster.

You see, I wasn't honest with myself. I thought I'd thrive without a box. I felt I was mature enough to succeed in a loose environment. I believed I'd become the kind of professional who could lead by example. The reality turned out to be that without a clock telling me what to do and when to do it, not enough got done.

I wasn't in a store *every single day*. I wasn't taking inventories *every single day*. I wasn't checking in on my teams *every single day*. This stemmed, in part, from the fact that there was barely any oversight. My only boss was thousands of miles away, and I didn't have anybody watching over my shoulder . . . and twentysomething John Gafford needed a shoulder-watcher. When it dawned on me how badly I was messing up—when I realized that I'd lied to myself, and that I'd approached this new sense of professional freedom without a plan or a goal—well, that was a huge revelation. This did eventually lead to me stepping down from that position in a too-little-too-late scenario, but, hey, I was learning,

Today, I'm so comfortable and successful working for myself that I could never again have a boss. It took decades for me to get to this point—getting completely free of The Drift takes way more than a few months or a couple of years—but making plans, setting goals, and internal honesty brought me closer to the finish line. I haven't yet crossed the finish line, and I never will, because once you consider the race done, you'll stop moving. And I'll never stop moving.

One of the best ways to stay on track is to get your own project manager. Your initial thought on this particular suggestion might be, *Dude, I can't afford to pay a project manager their going rate of between $74,000 and $120,000.*

Trust me, you can afford a project manager. You probably already have one.

When I was running our insurance agency in Florida, one of my salesmen was crushing it, so much so that he became the top salesman in Tampa. Suddenly, out of nowhere, I noticed that this guy, instead of going to his scheduled appointments, was playing golf, and going out for long lunches, and blowing off meetings, and generally half-assing his gig. Even though he was my best salesperson, I was being forced to do the responsible thing and fire him.

The problem was, this was my company.

And that screwup was me.

I was the CEO. I was the marketing department. I was the salesperson. I was *everything*. So John the CEO needed to fire John the salesperson, because John the salesperson was screwing around at the Bay Palms Golf Complex and not working leads.

I was part of the problem. But, eventually, I was the solution.

Once I figured out that whole mess, I realized that in order to properly plan for the company's future, I needed a project manager, a middle management entity who'd make sure I showed up where and when I needed to show up, that I returned phone calls and emails, that I didn't crater the company.

So I brought aboard a project manager in the form of a smartphone.

My smartphone became my lifeline, my companion, my savior. It told me how, when, and where to take care of my business. It reminded me of my daily commitments, and it didn't take no for an answer. If my phone told me I had to be somewhere at two, I'd be there at two, even if I was offered a free round of golf, because you can't argue with a goddamn phone.

This little rectangular project manager can also help your non-business life. If you have goals that involve your family, share them with your family via text. If you have plans with your wife, or your kids, or your wife *and* kids, drop them in the family calendar. And when those notifications pop up, don't disregard them. After all, why have your own personal project manager if you ignore them when they're trying to manage your projects?

Yeah, yeah, I know that a smartphone is an inanimate object, and it can't actually manage your projects, but it can offer you everything you need to know about the project in question. It can't do the job for you; all it can do is point you in the right direction.

But it can't give you the win.

If you're planning to win, you have to go into any situation—be it business or personal—with as much control as possible. But you must realize that the only thing you can truly 100 percent control is *you*. You see, with this system, I didn't make a choice every time something popped up on my calendar, but rather I committed to *one* thing, doing whatever popped up on my calendar whether I had better options or not. Once it made it in my phone, it was the law. Thinking like this made it much less overwhelming and much easier to commit.

In 2022, a real estate investing expert named Cody Sperber called me and said, "I'd like you to speak at my next conference." This was a huge deal. Cody ran one of the biggest real estate conferences in the country—we're talking as many as two thousand bodies. He added, "And I'd like Nick to join you. You guys can do a segment about flipping."

Nick was Nick Marietta, a gentleman with whom I was flipping luxury houses. I told Cody, "Whatever you need, man, I got you. No big deal; I'll take care of it."

At that point, I'd been on plenty of big stages, and I had no problem with my public speaking, but I had no clue as to whether or not Nick had any stage experience. So I called him up and said, "Buddy, we have this opportunity to speak at Cody's conference. First of all, do you want to do it?"

He said, "Yes, I want to do it. Very much."

I said, "Great," then asked, "Have you ever done anything like this?"

"No," he said. "I've never been on a stage before."

Uh-oh.

The more I thought about it, the more concerned I became. Aside from the fact that Nick had zero experience behind a microphone, it dawned on me that since there would be two of us there, this wasn't going to be a talk, but rather a play in which we'd both have preplanned interaction and lines, as well as some kind of stage directions.

Public speaking by yourself is hard; acting in a play with a non-actor is even harder. But I'd committed, so I had to figure it out, to make a plan. I decided that the best move was to divide and conquer: I could talk structure and be the host and interview Nick about construction, then I could wrap things up. My goal, aside from delivering a kick-ass presentation, was to make it as easy on Nick as possible.

The day of the presentation, Nick wasn't in a great space. While we were waiting in the wings, he kept saying stuff like, "I'm so nervous," and "I'm going to blow it," and "What am I doing here?"

He was terrified he was going to tank. I was terrified that the three thousand people out there were going to witness a train wreck. But we were there, and we had no choice but to go for it, so after we were introduced, we trudged onto the stage. Immediately, my nerves made my throat clench up to the point that I had to request a bottle of water before I could choke out a sentence. I felt like I'd swallowed a gallon of mothballs. (You can probably find a video of the talk online. You might not notice that I was having a throat problem, but I sure as hell did.) After all that, we got on with the presentation, and, all things considered, Nick did a hell of a job. I doubt that anybody in the audience had any idea that it was his first time doing something like that.

The point of all this is, I was so concerned about how Nick was going to perform that it affected my own performance. So when you're planning something, *anything*, if there are other people involved, make sure they can help you reach your goals. If you're too dependent on others, or too worried about what they're going to do, you'll be adversely impacted, the whole plan will suffer, and the chances of reaching your goal are significantly diminished.

Admittedly, when you work with somebody, you have to deal with the X factor, that X factor being their approach to your project. As noted, *you* can control *you*, but *you* can't control *them*. What you *can* do, however, is plan for all contingencies, to figure out the best- and worst-case scenarios and prepare for all eventualities.

So always embrace a safety net.

The good thing about today's work world is that there are numerous opportunities to overcome these sorts of snafus. If you're having negative experiences realizing your dreams alongside a partner or partners, do your own thing... and that thing can come via a side hustle.

A side hustle is a fantastic way to escape The Drift. Now driving an Uber is a perfectly solid side hustle... but don't you want *your* side hustle to be *your* side hustle? Don't you want to start a business of your own?

Right about now, you're thinking, *You bet I do, John! I'd love my own thing, something that I can grow into something like your thing!*

To that I'll say, *Glad to hear it! What's your plan?*

You might then say, *I don't know. Do I have to write a business plan or something?*

I'll say, *That's a great place to start.*

You'll say, *But aren't business plans hard?*

I'll say, *They can be. But they don't have to be.*

I've read my fair share of business plans—as you can tell, I appreciate a good plan—and the majority of them are thirty-plus pages long, and *very* elaborate.

I've also written my fair share of business plans—as noted, I appreciate a good plan—but none of them have run more than one page.

One page. One. Single. Page.

Because if I can't explain my concept in a single page, it's probably not worth explaining.

Many of the long, exhaustive business plans I've read have a section about why a large loan is necessary to launch, and there will be a long-winded, self-indulgent executive summary, and a whole bunch of other bullshit that doesn't actually have anything to do with bringing your concept to life. For me, that doesn't work. I want my quickie plan to quickly lay out the business's paradigm, its goals, and how the plan will be executed. For the most part, nothing else is necessary, so you can't let the traditional business plan model put the kibosh on your side hustle.

It goes like this . . .

Start with a mission statement, the who, what, where, when, and why of You Incorporated. Think about for whom you are doing this, when you plan to do it, why you are you doing it, and how you plan to do it.

If you don't have a mission statement, you don't have a mission. Just look at Harley-Davidson's mission statement: *More than building machines, we stand for the timeless pursuit of adventure. Freedom for the soul.* It's not, *We make good motorcycles.* No, it's inspirational. It's aspirational. And it's cool. Granted, they probably had a team of forty copywriters working on it for six months, but don't let that dissuade you from succinctly putting your own vision on paper.

Next should be your vision statement. Think of this as a destination on a map, where you're trying to go and what your life's going to look like when you get there. It should have a definitive time in the future, and a description of your life explaining why you're doing this in the first place, which will keep you motivated to get there. For example:

On December 31, 2028, I will own five rental properties generating $3,000 a month. I have saved $18,000 in my child's college fund. I am relaxed; I'm not worried about my finances.

Notice there is a definitive time in the future, and it's written in the present tense. This should become a mantra for you, because what we tell ourselves has a better chance of becoming reality.

You should also include your working financial goals. It can be units sold, dollars earned, services rendered, or anything you want, but it does have to be measurable and at least somewhat definitive.

Next step comes strategies, and you're only allowed to pick three, because I've found that most people just can't focus on more than three things at once.

When choosing your strategies, two of them should be tried-and-true, and one of them can be an idea, like something you want to try just to see if it works, just for the helluvit. The key to understanding what works and what doesn't is data, so if you're going to commit to a business plan, you must commit to tracking everything. As I'm fond of saying, "The truth is in the math. The data will tell us what to do."

That all being the case, let's pretend we're real estate agents and let's say the three strategies we are going to use for this quarter are:

- Internet leads
- Open houses
- Mailers

Under each strategy, you're going to develop *action steps,* the key to which is reverse engineering the steps from your goal, then making sure they're actionable and can be transferred into your daily calendar. Once your plan is in motion, you'll know exactly what you're supposed to be doing each week, each day, each hour.

Let's start with reverse engineering a goal and let's say the strategy is "Cold Calling." If you've never used this strategy before, you don't know the math it takes to procure a sale. You need to ask someone who has done this and use their data, while subtracting a 25 percent success ratio to account for your learning curve.

Let's say your goal is to make $40,000 this quarter, and every time you sell a product you make $10,000. To sell one unit, you have to go on five appointments. To get one appointment you have to make four hundred calls.

So $40,000 = 4 sales = 20 appointments = 8,000 calls.

Now that may seem daunting at first, but consider that there are twelve weeks in a quarter; that's approximately 666 calls over three days of a five-day workweek, which shakes out to approximately 222 calls a day. Now it's reasonable. Daunting, but reasonable.

So my action plan under the strategy would look something like this:

Mondays: Get new leads from your providers by noon and load into dialer.

Tuesdays: Between 9:00 AM and 1:00 PM, make your 222 calls.

Wednesday: Between 3:00 PM and 7:00 PM, make your 222 calls.

Thursday: Between 11:00 AM and 3:00 PM, make your 222 calls.

Friday: Follow up on the positive calls.

I can repeat this process for my other two strategies, making sure that the action plans don't overlap on my calendar. Then I transfer everything from this into my phone, and I know exactly what I'm supposed to do every single day.

Between my project manager, my innate desire to avoid sinking back into The Drift, and the need to take care of my family, all of this—the business plan, the daily grind—isn't just doable; it's enjoyable. And if you take it to heart, you'll have yourself an awesome, readable business plan.

This isn't to say that all these approaches are foolproof. There are a shit-ton of variables in business, so something that worked in 2021 might be useless today. As a result, you have to try new moves every quarter. If one of these moves succeeds, great, add it to your repertoire. If it doesn't work, get rid of it and go back to one of your tried-and-trues. You've got to constantly be evolving your business to account for new trends, new ideas, new interest, and new market conditions. That's how you stay ahead of the game.

When it comes to realizing my goals, I will admit that I get impatient, but sometimes in the real estate world, patience has to not only be acknowledged and accepted, but embraced. In my business—or in any sales situation, for that matter—there's a cycle. In my case, that means just because you ink a deal today doesn't mean you'll get paid tomorrow, because, for the most part, real estate deals don't close for thirty days, or forty days, or sixty days after the contract is signed. This becomes an issue if you've set time-sensitive goals, for example, *I'm going to pull in $40,000 in Q2.* Sometimes the timing doesn't jibe with your plans, and you have to consistently roll with that, or else you might get frustrated and quit. You'll use the fact that you didn't hit your mark as a mental crutch, as an excuse to give up.

The good news is that there's a way to avoid this cycle: Set your goals based on actions that are instantaneously measurable. For instance, I'll tell my team, "I don't care when the deal *closes.* I care about when it *opens,* so make it your goal to bring home X number of deals per quarter." Keeping tallies of openings rather than closings allows my people to be motivated till 11:59 PM on the final day of the quarter.

If you're going to hit your quarterly goals, or yearly goals, or lifetime goals, you need to stay organized. (This should go without saying. But I'm going to say it anyhow.) Me, I love a preplanned day supported by a quality checklist. If you're stuck in The Drift, put things in your calendar, and not just big stuff. Schedule your whole day, and—this is key—*stick to your damn schedule.* If you lay out a goal road map, give the road map to your project manager (aka, your smartphone). But if you consistently ignore it, you're Drifting. And if you *don't* ignore it, your life will be immeasurably better. Not only will you be more efficient in business, and not only will you have the satisfaction of checking stuff off your list, but you'll likely be able to carve out time for, say, the gym.

I also love tracking progress, so when you make your quality checklist, *use it*. Check off the completed tasks so you can pat yourself on the back and say, "I checked off my completed tasks, now I can bang out *another* checklist with *more* tasks that will take me to the next level." Because nothing is more motivating than seeing yourself make progress in real time.

I'm also a fan of using visual documentation as a motivator, whether it's a photo of your waistline or a screenshot of your bank account. If you snap a picture of your tummy in October, and it's tighter in December, success. If you track your bank account for six months, you'll have concrete proof that you're taking care of your business.

I'm well out of The Drift, but I still utilize visual tracking. An example: Credit Karma. I have great credit—it took me years to get there, but I made it—but even though my credit is solid, I still visit Credit Karma every week, without fail, in order to proudly gaze at their graphs. I've been doing that for years, and it still motivates me to keep my house in order. As someone who owns a mortgage company, I know these CK numbers aren't *exactly* right, but watching that graph is addictive.

Listen, none of this is easy—for that matter, setting and realizing goals is one of the most difficult aspects of escaping The Drift. You can hop aboard the goals-and-plans train, but to make the ride worthwhile, you have to get obsessed about it.

You have to be Michael Jordan.

You have to be Kobe Bryant.

Like them, you have the ability to thrive in any situation, but you won't thrive unless you make thriving a priority. MJ and Kobe prioritized being the best basketball player in the world, and while they both had the natural talent, they were also obsessive gym rats. They worked to improve their game each and every season, even after they'd won multiple scoring titles and championships. They were the gold standard—or, in MJ's case, the red-and-black standard—and they knew that unless they kept their goals at the forefront of their minds, the Nick Andersons and Eric Snows of the world would take them down.

And I don't know about you, but I'd rather be Kobe Bryant than Eric Snow.

CHAPTER 8

OVERCOMING PROCRASTINATION, DEVELOPING DISCIPLINE, AND FINDING MOTIVATION

EH, I'LL WRITE THIS CHAPTER TOMORROW

I was a child of the 1980s, and like far too many '80s kids, there wasn't a whole lot of structure to my childhood. I was raised by a working single parent and was thus often left to my own devices. I'm not complaining—I turned out okay, and without that sometimes-wobbly upbringing, you probably wouldn't be reading and enjoying the very book you're holding in your hands.

That said, flying (more or less) solo when you're a kid can go one of three ways:

1. You can end up with an unshakable sense of resilience.
2. You can get stuck in The Drift.
3. You can Drift, then try to escape The Drift using your dormant sense of resilience.

Me, I'm number three. As you likely guessed, my resilience didn't manifest itself until later in life, but when it did, man, did it come in handy.

When I tested for *The Apprentice*, Liza Siegel, the head psychologist on the show—who went on to write a fantastic book of her own called *Suite Success: The Psychologist from* The Apprentice *Reveals What It Really Takes to Excel—in the Boardroom and in Life*—told me that I'd tested higher for resiliency than anybody they'd ever had on the show. That's a lovely compliment, because at that point in my life, I was, to an extent, still Drifting, so hearing that from Liza told me I was heading in the right direction.

I think my resilience stems, in part, from my childhood; if you have a complete lack of structure, if you're left to your own devices, you have no choice *but* to be resilient. It's nice to know that this nonstandard upbringing led to me having this quality of which I'm so proud.

On the other hand, without this upbringing, I probably would've been better about showing up for places on time. In a nutshell, when I was Drifting, I had a punctuality problem... that problem being *I wasn't punctual.*

I don't have numbers to back this up, but from what I can tell, adults who trend toward procrastination didn't have a lot of structure growing up; they, like me, were always winging it. So I believe that procrastination is, to an extent, the result of a lifetime of winging it.

Remember a few pages back when I dropped that little anecdote about me firing myself? Well, one of the reasons I had to let myself go was because I was consistently late for meetings, that is, once I started raking in the bucks. As my sales figures skyrocketed, my punctuality plummeted.

If you're running a company, and you want to give it a better chance of sustaining itself, one of your prime objectives should be to maintain its integrity. Say you have a high-caliber performer on your staff, an employee who is unable to arrive where they need to be, when they need to be there. That makes the company look bad, and since the buck stops where the buck stops, it also makes the boss look bad. If the high performer can't turn it around after a couple of tough discussions, you've got to let them go, even if it's you.

To this day, I'm thrilled that I was able to identify my shortcomings and fire myself. (Quick aside: You can't underestimate the importance of self-awareness, because one of the most prevalent symptoms of The Drift is a notable lack of that quality.)

The primary way I was able to dig myself out of this procrastination hell was by implementing *systems*, because, as I came to learn, a system is the mortal enemy of procrastination. One system is relying on that project manager of yours.

I noted the importance of leaning on your smartphone's calendar, but I'll add to that by stating the obvious: *Lean harder*. Don't think of your upcoming appointment as an appointment, but rather a speed bump. Framing it this way means it doesn't come from a negative perspective—speed bumps save lives, and we should embrace them, even if they're a pain in the ass when we're trying to get somewhere on time. (See what I did there?)

If it's eleven o'clock and you get a calendar notification about your eleven-thirty meeting, *slow down*. That scheduled meeting, whether it's with a colleague, a potential client, a possible business partner, or a family member, takes precedence over anything. (Okay, let's amend that to say *precedence over anything within reason.*) You've committed your time, so follow through on the commitment. Even if you think it's the dumbest meeting in the history of dumb meetings, be there, and be there on time. If you consistently plant these speed bumps for yourself, this sort of punctual, responsible approach to your business life will become second nature.

If your phone's calendar isn't sufficient—if you're still late for stuff even after incorporating mental speed bumps into your life—there are always cutting-edge apps and programs popping up that will make your days more efficient. I dig one called Motion AI, and I'm not endorsing it, per se, just letting you all know that I use it, and I like it. Motion AI allows you to create links for the many tasks you perform during the day, the week, and the month. For example, if somebody wants to schedule time with you, the app sends a link that allows them to schedule time on your calendar. The magic of the app is that you can sync it with your to-do list, and next thing you know, your day and your tasks are all laid out in an easy-to-digest manner, and you barely had to lift a finger to make it happen.

All this said, if you're a heavy, chronic, Drifting procrastinator, the best smartphone and the coolest app aren't going to help you get to your 4:00 at 3:55. You have to *want* to get to your meetings five minutes early. And that's all about developing a discipline muscle. My way of amping up my level of discipline might not work for you—only you can figure out your best motivator—but for me, developing that muscle involved... developing muscles.

When I saw pictures of myself from my fiftieth birthday party, I was not happy with how they looked. I was heavier than I wanted to be, and my skin tone wasn't great, and I looked notably older than fifty. I thought, *Damn, I've got to get serious about taking care of myself. I've only got so many years left on this planet, and I'd like to try to stretch that as much as I can.* When you start seeing Facebook pages from people who you went to high school with—*and they've died*—you can't *not* contemplate your mortality.

Not to be morbid, but if you had to tell somebody that you have a week left on this planet, who would you call, and what would you do? I guarantee you wouldn't sit around trying to get to level nine on *Call of Duty*. But the reason that becomes an option is because you feel like you have all the time in the world. And the reality of it is you have no idea when your time is up. As Charles Barkley always says, "Father Time is undefeated."

Anyhow, remember my $50 Fit Club? In terms of improving my health and dropping a few pounds in the process, the club wasn't entirely sufficient—but it took me months, if not years, to figure out what *would* suffice. Trainers coming to the house wasn't the answer, nor were regular trips to the gym. Finally, when I felt my fifty years on Earth was having a negative impact on my body and mind, I stumbled onto something that resonated.

Naturally, it came courtesy of my project manager.

There are dozens of fitness apps available for download on your smartphone. Some of them are fantastic (not naming names), while others are garbage (again, not naming names), but you need to hit and miss in order to find the one that works for you. My go-to fitness app (again, not naming names) is typical in that it tracks your workouts, your caloric intake, and your weight, but I happen to like the interface. I appreciate the way it counts my reps, and schedules my water breaks, and allows me to check things off. (To reiterate, I like checklists.) Again, *my* perfect app might not be *your* perfect app, so try them all until you land on the one that helps you get into tip-top shape and improve your level of discipline. Because if you become disciplined enough to crush your workouts, you'll be disciplined enough to crush your schedule, and you get the rush of accomplishing what you needed to accomplish.

This sort of life change doesn't happen immediately after you download the right app or figure out the right system. For me, it's always been helpful to chart the results of any new life approach. If you're working on your weight, roll like that aforementioned minor league baseball team and photographically document your progress. When I'm in one of my more-than-a-little-periodic weight-loss stretches, I like to do that weekly, so when I look less saggy in week six than I did in week one, I'll be catapulted through to week nine, and week fourteen, and week fifty-two, and, hopefully, year seven. When my wife tells me, "Whoa, you can really see a difference," that's the best reward and the best motivator possible.

To that end, developing the discipline muscle goes hand in hand with swelling your motivation muscle. It bears repeating that goals and plans are far more likely to come to fruition when there's an underlying motive, whether that motive is rooted in family, or finances, or physicality.

If you don't have an innate sense of motivation, digging out of the procrastination hole—and out of The Drift—is that much more difficult. You have to find that pressure point because, well, don't you want to watch your kid walk down the aisle? If you do, let's talk about causality: If you can't show up somewhere on time, you're less likely to hold down a job. If you can't hold down a job, you're less likely to be a successful parent. If you're not a successful parent, you're less likely to see your kid walk down the aisle.

See? Causality.

One of the underlying causes of chronic lack of punctuality is a chronic lack of accountability. If you're having trouble getting things done, or sticking to your exercise plan, or balancing your budget, get an accountability partner. (Actually, if you're *really* having trouble getting things done, get two, or three, or ten accountability partners.) It doesn't have to be a professional coach, or a psychiatrist. It can be your spouse. It can be your kid. Hell, it can be literally anybody you trust.

What you do is tell your accountability partner, "Hey, I really want to accomplish this goal, and I want you—no, I *need* you—to hold me accountable, so I want you to check on me every week and make sure I did what I was supposed to do." (Before you hire your spouse for the job, you better be damn sure that you're ready to make these life changes; otherwise, you're going to start to view them as a nag rather than as a partner. They also won't be too thrilled with you.)

Accountability isn't always a work thing—you also have to be accountable for the words that come out of your mouth. For instance, anytime I hear my kids say, "I *have* to go to practice," I immediately stop them and say, "No, you *get* to go to practice. Because there are a lot of people on this planet who would give anything to be able to go and do what you're doing right now. You're lucky to have been born into a home where not only can you practice, but you have loving parents who support whatever it is you're practicing for."

You also must be careful about the labels that come out of your mouth, because sometimes a label offers an excuse for bad behavior—and this is exceedingly prevalent among millennials.

If I had to guesstimate, the biggest Drift demographic is the generation that was born between 1981 and 1996. Bear with me while I make some sweeping generalizations, but from my experience, in a professional environment, millennials question *everything*: "How long is this going to take? How hard will I have to work? When can I shut it down for the day?" And you know who's the worst about stereotyping millennials? That's right, millennials themselves. They'll shrug off some traditional millennial behavior by saying, "What can I say, I'm a millennial." They label themselves, and that label gives them, in their mind, a reasonable excuse to blow off meetings, to be late for work, to do a half-assed job, and to complain, complain, complain.

There are plenty of other labels that get used as excuses, some of which are even more ridiculous than the millennial thing. Back in my restaurant days, during our pre-shift meetings, we'd play a game called Horoscope / Not Your Horoscope. I'd ask one of the servers, "What's your sign?"

She might say, "Sagittarius."

Then I'd open up the newspaper to the horoscope page and read aloud something like, "Take up new responsibilities at the workplace. Today, your finance is a mixed bag. Health is also normal. Ensure you spend more time with your lover and handle the official responsibilities diligently."

She'd then inevitably say, "Oh my God, that's *so* me!"

I'd look at her and think, *No. It's not. You're irresponsible, and you already spend way too much time with your lover and that was the Aries horoscope for the day.*

Admittedly, I was playing this game primarily to tease the girls, and to call bullshit on horoscopes. (I was a little bit of an asshole then, but a goodly percentage of Drifters have plenty of asshole in them.) But it's the same thing with any label. It doesn't matter what month you were born. It doesn't matter what year you were born. Life is oftentimes about the choices that you make and how they affect your future. And when you start applying labels to yourself in an attempt to make up for bad behavior, or a crappy performance—or a *non*performance—you're setting yourself up for failure.

To that end, I recently stumbled onto an Instagram video made by a young woman who, while driving a car, screamed about her parents for two minutes straight—parents who, as she explained, had worked in factories their whole lives and who told her to go to college, and when she graduated, she'd be able to do whatever she wanted. She paused, then discussed how she'd graduated school, but now she was in debt and couldn't find a job. Her parents, in an effort to help, suggested she go to trade school, which deeply offended her.

And she deeply offended me.

She blamed her parents for her current situation, which is utter bullshit. If I ever ran into her, I'd ask, "What did you do while you were in college? What did you study? Did you study something that was going to be useful to the world?" Then I'd say, "I'm sure that when you were in school, you didn't stay home every night. I'm sure you didn't work at a restaurant forty hours a week while you were acing your homework. At times, you probably funneled beer on the porch of a frat house, and now you're bitching on social media because you don't have a good job? And you're blaming your parents? Who footed the bill for your schooling, and offered you a logical suggestion for moving forward?" Then I'd finish it off with, "Procrastination and personal accountability go hand in hand. I find the people who get the least done have the most people to blame for it. So get it together."

I have a confession: Mild versions of this sort of behavior can be found in the Gafford household. When asked to clean her room, my daughter will procrastinate, and procrastinate, and procrastinate some more. At which point we'll gently remind her to clean up. After that, we'll not-so-gently remind her to clean up.

At which point, she'll say, "Oh, I'm just a messy girl."

This happened a lot. So one day, I snapped a little bit and said, "You're not messy. You're inconsiderate." Her eyes got really big as I continued, "You're inconsiderate because you just assume that your mother's going to clean up after you. Don't ever call yourself messy again. Call yourself inconsiderate because that's how you're acting."

I thought I handled it perfectly. I didn't yell. I didn't scream. But I got my point across in a way that, considering how much her eyes widened, I thought had resonated with her.

It didn't. She's still messy as hell. But she's a kid and an awesome one at that, so she gets somewhat of a pass.

Along those lines, if or when you're late, and you blame it on the fact that you're always late and that's just who you are, I'll tell you, "You're not always late. You just don't care about other people's time." And since I have zero tolerance for listening to lame excuses for lame behavior, I won't use the relatively gentle tone I used with my daughter.

I'll credit (or blame) an old partner who shall remain nameless for my annoyance with a lack of punctuality and accountability. The guy was a narcissist who expected the world to bend to his schedule. He always said, "I'm always late," but he just didn't have any consideration for anyone else's time. This meant we were late for everything, and he embarrassed me over and over again.

This is probably why, to this day, lateness from others eats at me so much.

One of my favorite lessons about being on time is from my colleague Gavin, a fantastic business partner and one of the top luxury listing agents in Nevada. In Gavin's listing classes, if an agent walks in thirty seconds late, Gavin tells him, "If this was a listing appointment and you showed up thirty seconds late, you've lost the listing." Then he throws them out of the class to emphasize his point.

That may sound harsh, but that's how the world works. Like the immortal Ricky Bobby said, "If you ain't first, you're last."

Sometimes chronic lack of punctuality, no accountability, and little motivation come about through no fault of your own. Sometimes, it's about brain chemistry.

I suffer from seasonal affective disorder, which manifests itself via depressive episodes brought on by a change in season. It happens once or twice a year. I call it The Funk. I'm a super-high-energy guy, but when The Funk hits, it's hard for me to even get out of bed. Even though I realize what's going on, I still don't want to get up and do anything. But I never say die, and one way I'm able to pull myself out of it is to *think small.*

When I find myself in one of these depressive states, I'll grab my smartphone, go to my fancy calendar app, look at my to-do list, and pick one item, just one. And if I can get that one thing done, that'll give me a modicum of momentum, which makes me want to lean into that momentum and check off another task. And another. And another. On the first day of The Funk, I might only accomplish that one task, but when it comes to depression, any kind of forward movement is crucial. The task in question can be as easy as returning a phone call. It can be as simple as paying a bill. It can be as small as washing my socks. It doesn't have to be something monumental—it just has to be *something*, as long as it gets the ball rolling. Eventually, the completed tasks will pile up and, next thing you know, you've run through a chunk of your list, and your work is nudging you out of your Funk, and you didn't even realize it.

Another way to help alleviate potential Funk issues is to get dressed. Seems simple, but when you're Funked Up, it's not.

Real estate has gotten a little bit more casual over the years, and there's a pretty good chance that not everyone at my companies will be dressed in a suit. I'm fine with that, but there's a time and a place for everything, and sometimes, showing up on time isn't good enough. Sometimes, you need to play the part, and playing the part generally means putting on a costume.

You don't believe me? Well, think about Superman.

Superman doesn't jump out of the phone booth wearing what Clark Kent wore to work—he changes into a Superman suit. And there's something about putting on a Superman suit—or, in our case, some nice work clothes—that leads to a positive mental shift. When you look in the mirror and see somebody who looks like a businessperson, it's hard not to act like a businessperson.

I remember one afternoon, one of my salespeople strolled into the office wearing head-to-toe sweats. I said, "Ummm, that's a look. Pretty casual."

He said, "It's cool. I don't have any appointments today."

I looked him up and down, then said, "Do you think you're dressed for the day that you have or the day that you *want* to have? Because in this business, in real estate, you never know. Your phone could ring right now, and you'll have to go do something that requires you to, you know, *not be in sweats*."

I'm not saying that every day is a suit day, but if you work in a consumer-facing environment, every day should *not* be a sweats day.

Of equal importance, if you're someone who doesn't currently have a job, wake up every single day and get dressed as though you were going to work. Treat your job hunt as a job. Set an alarm. Look presentable. *Set* your hours and *keep* your hours, whether it's nine-to-five, or ten-to-six, or sunrise-to-sunset. If you put yourself in the mindset of somebody who's employed, it'll make you that much more employable.

If this all sounds difficult, that's only because it is, especially if you've lived a life lacking motivation and accountability. And part of the difficulty stems from repetition.

Putting on a suit is boring. Your commute is boring. The boring parts of your job are, naturally, boring. These are among the dozens of things that happen in your professional life each and every day: Lather, rinse, repeat. But, more often than not, repetition leads to results.

Finally, I'm going to button up this discussion with an anecdote about my son, a bright kid who has justifiable Ivy League aspirations. In his honors geometry class this year, he had to get an 87 on his final to get an A and maintain his GPA. If he got a B, his top ten schools were off the table.

One day, I asked him how the studying for the test was progressing. I wasn't being nosy or naggy, just parentally curious.

He said, "I'll start tomorrow."

I then became naggy. "It's Friday," I said. "The test is Monday. Maybe you should start studying now."

He repeated, "I'll start tomorrow."

Next day, same thing: "I'll start tomorrow."

Then Sunday night rolls around. It's seven thirty and he comes into my office, freaking out. "I can't figure out how to do some of this stuff!"

I said, "You're discovering this now? Like eighteen hours before the test?"

"Can you help?"

I'm not exactly an Alan Turing–like numbers wiz, so we scrambled around to find an AI math tutor. He studied all night, and while he landed his A—his score was 90.1, so it was damn close—there's no reason it should've gotten to that point. I remind him of this every time he has a test coming up—he's not perfect at studying right away, but he always learns from his mistakes.

Listen, I get that it's not easy to make these sweeping life changes, whether you've been Drifting for one year, or five years, or ten years, or your entire life. Doing *exactly* what you have to do *when* you have to do it can be difficult, exhausting, and just plain no fun; I think most of us will agree it's far more enjoyable to hit the snooze button than it is to hustle to an 8:00 AM breakfast meeting. But if you can't shake this sort of behavior—if you can't figure out how to be punctual each and every day—you'll eventually snooze yourself out of jobs, friends, and victories.

Personally, I enjoy victories rooted in punctuality and accountability, so I like what Michael Jordan's trainer Tim Grover once said: "If you think the price of winning is too high, wait until you get the bill from regret."

CHAPTER 9

MANAGING RISK

DON'T FEAR THE FLORIDA SNOW

There's risk. And there's risk.

For the sake of this discussion, the first type of risk is inherent risk, the kind of risk where you think, *I'm Drifting, but I'll take a chance that the planets will align, and my dream job—a job that pays me six figures and allows me to take a five-hour nap in the middle of the day—will fall into my lap without me even having to look for it, and then I'll find a three-bedroom apartment on the Upper West Side for six hundred dollars a month, and then I'll meet the mate of my dreams at Starbucks, and they'll take me out to a fancy dinner at Per Se, and they'll become my sugar mama/daddy, and I'll be set for life, so I'm going to take a risk that this will all happen and continue not looking for a job, and keep up with my five-hour naps, and keep waiting for my school loans to be paid off by a wealthy individual.*

This approach to life is inherently risky and, to those of us who are anti-Drifters, annoying as hell. Drifters delude themselves into believing that they'll be fine if they continue to let the world happen to them, rather than try to bend the world to their will. Now you see why I want to put an end to Drifting.

The second type of risk is calculated risk, the type of risk that involves research, experience, and testicular fortitude...and, ladies, for the purpose of our discussion, you get to have your own brand of testicular fortitude. It's not just gauging which direction the wind is blowing; it's making your risk as logical as risk can be. (Risk and logic aren't necessarily kissing cousins, but you get the point.)

Even though I'm based in Las Vegas—a city where risk oozes out of every inch of the Strip—I avoid inherent risk at all costs. I'm not going to hit the casino and roll the dice and hope they land in a combination of numbers that will garner me enough chips to bend the world to my will. I might, however, consider doing a little bit of dice sliding. (If you're not familiar with dice sliding, please google it. I don't want to get tagged for teaching the world how to cheat at craps.) I wouldn't actually slide any dice—I have no clue how to do it; I'd just consider it—but that's a calculated risk, because you know the two outcomes: Either you'll win a bunch of money, or the pit boss will drag you off the casino floor to an exit, where he'll throw you through a plate glass window.

I wouldn't take that risk. But I'd consider it. Because calculated risk can be awesome.

One of the biggest calculated risks I ever took was when I auditioned for *The Apprentice*.

Man, that was a process. I had to fill out twenty-five or so applications that featured more or less the same questions, just written in a different way. I had to record multiple videos in which I sold myself. I had to go through an extensive—*very* extensive—background check. But I survived and made it to Finals Week, where I had to fly out to Los Angeles for a series of psychological evaluations, and IQ tests, and probing interviews, along with forty-nine other exhausted wannabe businesspeople.

Finals Week was... interesting. They took us to a hotel, the Embassy Suites in Santa Monica, where we were all given our own room and told that we could leave for meals and trips to the gym... and that was it. It was like being in the nicest jail in the world.

We *Apprentice* hopefuls ate meals together, but we weren't allowed to speak, because the producers wanted to document on camera the first time the final cast members officially met. The first day, there were fifty people in the restaurant. The next, forty. Then forty became thirty. As they cut people they sent them home, so every day I figured my odds of getting on the show got a little better.

One day, a casting PA came to my room and said, "Okay, man, we're going to go up and meet with Burnett. Today's Burnett Day. He's here. He's going to interview you, so try and be interesting."

No problem. I could be interesting.

Suited and booted up, I strolled through the double doors into a huge room, and there's Mark Burnett along with a bunch of NBC big muckety-mucks, maybe fifteen people in all.

I stuck out my hand and said, "My name is John Gafford."

Mark was popping peanut M&M's into his mouth, and rather than shake my hand, he plopped an M&M into my palm. I ignored the candy and spent the next ten minutes dropping all my amazing anecdotes, attempting to convince them how wonderful I was. (Confession: I did a fair amount of embellishing.) All Mark wanted to discuss was the fact that my friend Rick Wells—who I used as a reference—told somebody that my girlfriend was getting ready to dump me.

When I'm speaking in front of an audience, it's easy for me to tell when I'm losing them, and I knew that I'd lost this audience *immediately*. I could almost see Mark mentally shuffling through the other people who'd been in that room that day. I left the room knowing full well it had gone horribly, confident that I wouldn't be chosen.

Back in the suite, I started packing my bags and thought, *That was a good run. At least I have a cool story to tell my friends back home*. Before I could close my suitcase, the PA knocked on the door. "Mark wants to speak to you again," he said.

"Really?"

"Really."

Cool, I thought. *This time, I'm gonna do it my way.*

Before we left the room, I hit the minibar. When we got upstairs, I kicked open the doors—that's right, *kicked*—bulled into the room, and told Mark, "Buddy, before you make a decision on casting me on your little television show, here's what you need to know: When you invest in me, you'll get back one hundred times your initial investment." Then I took a bag of M&M's I had swiped from the minibar from my pocket, threw them in his face, and said, "Thanks for the fucking M&M's, Mark." And I walked out.

I wouldn't recommend using that approach next time you're trying to get a gig, but this wasn't a job interview—it was a casting call for a television show. In retrospect my approach was not that different from others. Ryan Serhant told a story on my podcast about his approach to casting with *Million Dollar Listing New York*. He straight-up snowed the casting people. He rented a Range Rover and a fake driver to run him all over New York while simultaneously taking planned fake phone calls from everyone he knew. Apparently yelling "*No, Yuri, the wire has not hit*" at your mother on your cell is about the same as tossing some candy-coated treats.

My mistake the first time in the room was treating the meeting like a typical job interview, but that was my poor analysis of the situation. When I realized they were looking for somebody who'd be compelling on camera, I took a calculated risk. I figured I'd already lost—I knew I was cooked, just *knew* it—so I had absolutely nothing to lose by going balls-out and trying to make a ruckus.

Turns out Mark Burnett *loves* ruckuses. My ruckus led to the biggest opportunity of my life, and had I not gone balls-out and landed the part—not the job, the *part*—who knows what would have happened?

When setting up a deal, you have to examine risk—while also spending time studying its periodic friend, reward—in order to determine what you stand to gain, what you stand to lose, and whether the potential gain mitigates the potential loss. Whenever I'm mulling a business deal, I ask myself, *What's the upside here?* But I also realize that I can't get so caught up in the upside that I make a haphazard decision. More importantly, I also consider the *downside* in an attempt to understand the potential harm, and whether or not I can live with a negative outcome.

Now the good news is, if you're reading this book, you're probably in a situation where if or when your deal goes south, you'll be able to recover; if you make one mistake, you're not going to lose a multibillion-dollar company. At that point, your downside becomes a matter of whether or not you can live with an unfavorable outcome, whether or not you can get past a bad decision.

Considering risk isn't just a business thing. Friendships can be risky. Love can be risky. Buying a car can be risky. But I've found that the price of *not* doing something is higher than the price of doing it. To revisit that Tim Grover quote, "If you think the price of winning is too high, wait until you get the bill from regret."

It could be argued that the biggest thing you need to consider when it comes to managing risk is who you're betting on. *Is the person in question trying to screw me over? Can they engage in a good faith negotiation? If we come to an agreement, will they live up to their end of the bargain? And can I pull this off?*

But the biggest, most important question is, *Do I want to bet on myself?*

To that, I offer a resounding, *Hell yeah.*

Nobody—*nobody*—is going to have your best interests at heart better than you. Nobody—*nobody*—knows your goals, hopes, and dreams better than you. Nobody—*nobody*—knows your level of risk aversion better than you.

That said, you don't need to take your risks all by your lonesome. For that matter, in some risky situations, finding the right partner is essential, mostly because it's always a good idea to have a trusted set of eyeballs go over a risky deal. You'll get a different perspective that could lead to an angle you might've missed, be it positive or negative. Your partner might find something that'll win you the negotiation—or something else that'll convince you to walk away from the bargaining table altogether. Besides, as the old proverb says, *If you want to go fast, go alone. If you want to go far, go together.*

Nick Daniel, one of the founders of the previously mentioned, wildly successful fitness app V Shred—an app I'm sure you've seen streaming down your social media—shared on my podcast a pivotal moment in the company's history:

> In the beginning of V Shred, Nick and his team were pushed to their limits, having burned their bridges to commit fully to their venture. Despite their efforts, after trying everything Nick knew to have been successful in prior start-ups in digital marketing, they found themselves teetering on the edge of failure. Financial losses were mounting, and their partner, Roger, even suggested that it might be the end of their endeavor.
>
> One day amidst this turmoil, Nick found himself overwhelmed. He went for a run, seeking solace, and

ended up on a park bench, where he broke down, feeling utterly defeated. It was in this moment of despair that he recalled videos he had seen online—hour-long pieces that he initially dismissed as ineffective. However, he remembered a conversation with his partner Kevin Pearn, who pointed out that these lengthy videos must be working, or else they wouldn't be so prevalent.

Fueled by this realization, Nick sprinted home, driven by a newfound determination. He scoured the Internet for these videos, which covered various topics like skincare. He hired a freelancer from India to transcribe them, and then he meticulously analyzed them, searching for the underlying formula that made them successful.

Nick's deep dive into the structure of these videos paid off. He identified key elements—the lead, the golden threads—and applied his findings to create V Shred's own version. He collaborated with Vince, their partner and spokesman, and other team members to integrate unique aspects of their fitness programs into the content.

Their hard work culminated in a make-or-break moment. With only $400 left in the bank, the team produced a video and corresponding ads. With the team agreement that this was a calculated risk, they launched their campaign and anxiously waited. The results were astonishing—an incredible 900 percent ROI [return on investment].

From there, it was a race against time and finances. They would spend all their available funds on ads, pause them to wait for the bank to clear the payments, and then start again. This strategy allowed them to gradually build their finances, from a mere $400 to a substantial $100,000.

Combined with the collective brain power of the entire team, this calculated risk paid off. As I write this, V Shred has done over $1.3 billion in sales, a testament to the power of resilience, the importance of innovative thinking, and the relentless pursuit of success against all odds.

When you're putting together a deal of *any* sort, risk is baked into the process. It's expected. That's also the case when you're attempting a different way of marketing yourself or your company. If your marketing plan sticks, your business can go to the next level. If it tanks, you probably won't go out of business, but you could look like an idiot.

Betting on yourself is all fine and good, but you also have to take into account that you can't control everything, which is why, when entering a potentially risky situation, make certain that you're at least 51 percent of the equation. To illustrate, let's take a time machine back to the early '90s and my stint at Tallahassee's Equator Café.

It was spring, and twenty-year-old me decides that this is the perfect time to host a Reggae Sunsplash event at the bar. "It's gonna be the bomb," I told the owners. "Nobody's ever done anything like this. I'm going to get these reggae bands from all over Florida, and we're gonna sell a shitload of drinks, and we're gonna get some loyal customers." After a pause, I repeated, "It's gonna be the bomb." (This was 1992, so it was perfectly reasonable for things to be "the bomb.")

The owners liked the idea and appreciated my enthusiasm, so they signed off on it.

I felt in my gut that hundreds of people would attend this thing, so step one was to make sure we had enough beer on hand. I bought one hundred kegs from Budweiser and, since we didn't have the refrigerator space and it was still a little cold out, I lined them up in an outdoor hallway.

After I finished procuring the liquor and booking the music, it dawned on me that this little Sunsplash of mine was an insanely big risk. It was a new endeavor, and there were bands coming in from all over the state, and there was a lot of inventory that needed to be moved. On the other hand, if I pulled it off, it would be the hugest thing the area had ever seen.

So the day of the party rolls around. The club looked immaculate. The beer was cold. The bands were ready to jam.

At which point, for the first time in twenty-one years, we looked up into the sky and saw... freakin'... *snow*. My Reggae Sunsplash became a Reggae Snowsplash. And who the hell wants to go to a Reggae Snowsplash in Tallahassee? Nobody, that's who. So we pulled the plug. (Actually, we'd barely plugged in at all, so plug-pulling was a formality.)

Budweiser was understanding about the situation and took back the extra kegs. All the bands but one were also understanding, happy to forgo their fee as long as we covered their transportation. (I made the one band that kicked up a fuss play their set... in the snow. I mean, they insisted on getting paid, so I insisted they play some music.)

The point of all this is, if you bring weather into the equation, your 51 percent control level goes out the window, because you have zero percent control of keeping snow or rain or a hail of frogs at bay. Nonetheless, if I were still running a club, I wouldn't be the least bit afraid to schedule another Sunsplash. I'd just take out a shitload of insurance, because a shitload of insurance allows me 100 percent control of the weather. Let it snow, I now say. Let it snow.

The Sunsplash mess didn't dissuade me from taking musical risks.

Real estate is a little subjective—we can all agree that a killer house is a killer house, but that particular killer house might not be killer for *you*. Art, on the other hand, is completely subjective—I don't love the Beatles, but you can't tell me I'm wrong, because even if you think I have bad taste, it's *my* taste. When it comes to music, there's no right or wrong. Knowing that, when it comes to taking a risk on an artist, sometimes you've just got to do whatever the hell you want, consequences be damned.

My friend Tom Drummond, bass player for the band Better Than Ezra, called me one day and said, "I found this kid in New Orleans. His name is Josh Martin. I want to make a record with him. I want to create a record label for this kid."

I trusted Tom's taste in music, so I asked him to send me some of Josh's stuff, and once I heard it, I said yes, and didn't care about getting paid. As a lifelong musician, I loved the idea that I could say that I owned a record label, even if we dropped just one record. That was so appealing to me that I didn't care if Josh went platinum. Still, if there was money to be made from the project, I wouldn't refuse it, so we signed him to a 360-management deal, which meant that if he *did* get signed by a major label and *did* go platinum, we'd all line our pockets.

The record dropped, and it was terrific, but Josh didn't get signed by a major label, nor did he go platinum, nor did we line our pockets...and I didn't care one bit. I didn't consider it a loss, and I still don't consider it a loss. I took a risk, and it didn't pay off financially. But my soul was enriched, and sometimes, if that's the outcome of a risky play, it's not just a loss.

It's a straight-up, inarguable win.

CHAPTER 10

BECOMING A BETTER YOU

CLEAN UP THE DISTORTION

I can hear some of you now.

"John, dude, listen, I'm not stuck. My life is totally together. I'm just reading this book because you seem like a good guy, and I thought it would be fun to hang out with you for 188 pages."

I appreciate the sentiment, but... that's a load of crap. We all have places we can improve.

If you've stuck with me this far, a part of you is well aware you've got some opportunity for growth. That part of you might be buried deep down in your psyche, or it might be mere millimeters from the surface. That part may be massive and that part may be tiny. Your instinct might be to ignore that part, but it's there, and you have to deal with it.

And deal with it head-on.

Remember that scene from the greatest Christmas movie of all time, *Die Hard*, the scene when John McClane (Bruce Willis) is asked by one of Hans Gruber's (Alan Rickman's) henchmen (no idea who played him, but it's not important, because he's a freakin' henchman), "Why don't you come out and join the others? No one is coming to help you"?

McClane was aware nobody was coming to help him—and he didn't care, because he knew he was a badass and had the tools to get out of the situation. Even though McClane was Drifting—just look at his marriage—when it came to saving Nakatomi Tower and all the useless hostages, he had enough wherewithal to realize *it was on him*. It was about coming to grips with the fact that the henchman was right: Sometimes no one is coming to help you.

Once you embrace that fact—and this is a fact you can and should embrace—you've taken a huge step toward long-term growth. You can get to the point where you *expect* help, and expecting help is a sure way to stunt any kind of growth.

Not getting this one concept held me in The Drift for much of my young life.

When I was a kid, I always thought I had a safety net, fully believing that if/when I got in trouble, my dad would bail me out. And money would never be an issue for me, because when my dad eventually retired or passed away, there'd be this giant nest egg with my name on it. That didn't happen. But due to my misguided beliefs in that area, I developed this need to let others take care of me, which caused problems in every aspect of my life.

Even when it came to dating.

I'd hop from relationship to relationship, never really pulling my weight. For instance, when I was in my early twenties, as was almost always the case when a relationship of mine reached *that level*, I'd move in with my girlfriend—but we'd never move into my place, only theirs. In a sense, I went from being cared for by my mother to getting help from another female caretaker. And another. And another. And another.

Accepting motherly support from a series of people who aren't your mother is as Drifty as it gets.

This type of dependency becomes a habit—most Drifters don't realize that it *is* a habit—and a problematic habit at that. See, the easiest way to dilute your sense of personal responsibility and stunt your personal development is to assume somebody else will always take care of you.

To reiterate Mr. Henchman's take on the whole thing: They won't.

And the sooner you accept that nobody's going to get it done for *you* except for *you*—that *your* responsibility is *your* responsibility—the quicker you'll put the brakes on your Drifting and see what *you* have under the hood.

Acknowledgment is a great place to start this journey:

- Acknowledge that your shortcomings and your maturity deficiency and your stubbornness are part of the reason you're Drifting.
- Acknowledge that you need to do some growing.
- Acknowledge that growing can be difficult and painful.
- Acknowledge that you're ready to do the work that will help you grow, help you walk on a solid surface, and help you become the best person—and best businessperson, for that matter—that you can be.

If you're not happy with the results, go back and do it all again. And again. And again. Deep dives into your psyche are never a bad thing.

The best part about this is when you start actively trying to improve your life by taking full responsibility for all your actions, others notice, and better yet—and somewhat ironically—some will *want* to help.

This isn't to say that I don't feel empathy for people in some form of need—I just have a different method of selecting who I will help. My default mode is to help those who I see have the desire and skills to help themselves—and if somebody genuinely wants to help themselves, I'm all in, and will do literally anything I can do to get them safely over the speed bumps. And when I say "literally anything," that means anything up to and including writing a book.

Case in point, as I write this I had two interviews yesterday for agents desiring to be on my personal real estate team. The first agent, whose name was Angel, had been working as a high-level inside sales associate for another luxury broker in town, setting appointments for that agent. That may sound simple, but that's literally the hardest part of what we do.

When I asked Angel why she wasn't interested in just working the leads all the way through, she said, "I don't have the confidence to go on these appointments by myself."

Confidence is something I can help fix, and I was ready and eager to do just that. She demonstrated the wherewithal to understand her shortcomings, which made her somebody I knew how to help.

As for the second agent, within the first three minutes of our conversation, she said, "My two years in real estate have been a failure because of my brokerage, and my broker, and her previous team leader . . ."

The list went on, and at no point did she take responsibility for her lack of production. (I know she told me this in the first three minutes because that's how long the interview lasted. *See you later, not interested.*)

I tend to hear a lot of odd things when interacting with people, but the oddest thing to me is that people love to label themselves.

I'm talking to you, millennials.

Too many millennials *love* to call themselves millennials, and they generally do so in the absolute worst context.

For instance, here's what I've cobbled together from lord-knows-how-many job interviews I've conducted with overly entitled thirty-year-olds:

What the Millennial Says: The millennial in me has to ask: How much time off will I get?

What I Hear: I'm super-lazy and looking to work as little as possible.

What the Millennial Says: The millennial in me needs to know what I'll get out of this company beyond my deserved salary.

What I Hear: As soon as someone opens a business with a Ping-Pong table in the break room, I'm out of here.

It's not so much the question that triggers my response—it's the label. Don't dump yourself in with a whole group of people. Be unique and, as Oscar Wilde is believed to have said, "Be yourself. Everyone else is taken."

I'm not just gonna pick on millennials here, as the same thought process goes along with any label you might bestow upon yourself. I'm too "old" to learn technology; I'm too "busy" to chase my dreams. I'm "stuck" in my current situation and there's no way out. I'm too "young" to be taken seriously.

A label gives that sort of statement power. If you remove the label, you remove the power.

Unless in certain instances when the label gives you power.

Like it does in the Gafford household.

I don't say this to stroke my ego, but in my household, having the label of being a Gafford means something. My wife and I make sure it does every day.

What it means to be a Gafford is to never squander an opportunity that's given, to appreciate the opportunities that you're given, and to do your best with those opportunities. I don't care if anybody else on the planet understands this...but I care that my two kids do.

As I write this, my sixteen-year-old son is prepping to have a kick-ass summer... and by that I mean he'll be kicking some ass while interning with some guys who run one of the biggest digital online media companies in the world. He'll be there every day, working side by side with the founders of a billion-dollar entity, learning how to be a world-class copywriter, and a world-class media buyer, and, well, a world-class everything. He'll develop the skills to build a $100 million dollar company. And he won't complain about anything.

Sure, he didn't land the gig in a vacuum—I hooked him up. But I gave him the help because I knew he'd accept it graciously and gratefully. And he accepted the help because he was ready for the help, because he was hungry.

From my perch, it feels like a lack of hunger—a dearth of desire—is a major issue with most Drifters, and they'd better get hungry, because they're going to get lapped by a Gen Z full of grinders and hustlers. They'll get outworked, outthought, outeverything'd.

This next generation of kids is here to win.

Labels can also change the world's perception of you, another reason they can be dangerous. For instance, back in the early aughts, if you went to a dinner party and told one of the guests, "I'm an entrepreneur," they might think, *Hah, entrepreneur probably means he doesn't have a job.*

Twenty years ago, they might have been right. Today, not so much. One pass through your LinkedIn feed tells us that entrepreneurs are today's rock stars.

The hustlers and grinders don't look to musicians or actors for inspiration, but rather to the GaryVees and the Grant Cardones. Gary and Grant are their Tom Cruise, their Jay-Z, their Kim Kardashian...and thank God, because that means Kim Kardashian isn't their Kim Kardashian.

I think the reexamination of the word *entrepreneur* comes from the acceptance that you can thrive without a degree from Harvard. Success is now seen as obtainable by anyone with this label. (Wow, that just fired me up!) And anyone can be a successful entrepreneur by following this formula:

Make a plan.

Figure out if you can execute the plan on your own.

If you can execute it, execute it.

If you can't, then ask *who, not how*.

Fill in the blind spots.

Work your ass off to bring your plan to fruition.

(Admittedly, a little luck is often necessary.)

As easy as that might seem, some people just can't get out of their own way. They'll blame their Driftiness on something that happened in the past, rather than realize their future has been in their hands the whole time.

Growing up, my wife's mother had it tough. Due to some adoption weirdness, she was raised like Cinderella; she was the stepchild who didn't receive the same love or care as the two blood daughters.

My wife didn't have what one might consider a normal childhood, primarily because her mother had no frame of reference regarding what it took to be a great parent. For example, birthdays and holidays were celebrated with an envelope of cash rather than a Christmas tree or a thoughtful card. It was like, *Here's some money; now let's get on with the day*. Without knowing she did it, my mother-in-law, to a certain degree, replicated her parenting example.

Conversely, my wife is the best mother ever. Before we had kids, she told me, "I'm going to be the peanut butter and jelly mom." And I knew exactly what she meant: She wanted our house to be the one where kids congregate and have fun and eat as much PB&J as their hearts desire.

And that's exactly what she is, so if you're ever in our neighborhood, chances are she'll make you a sandwich, too.

Without realizing it, my wife's mother helped my wife become the mother that she is—and this is an instance of getting help from somebody even though they weren't trying to help. The takeaway is that role models can be found in the oddest places and at the oddest times, so always, always, *always* pay attention.

In terms of wobbly upbringings, my wife is far from alone, and I can speak to that with authority, as I had parental issues of my own. (For more details, revisit chapter one. And chapter three. And chapter six. And maybe a little bit of chapter eight. Hell, just read the whole thing again.) Mom and Dad got divorced when I was about eight, plus my father wasn't around as much as he should've been; it felt like the only time I saw him was either when I went to his office after school, or when we went fishing or hunting. (Don't cry for me; later in life, he was a *much* better parent.)

I pride myself on being a great father to my kids, on being present, on being here, on being a part of things. The Gafford home is stable and loving—always was, always will be—in part because I chose to see my previous experience for what it was, and improve on it.

Your previous life experience shouldn't compel you to repeat the sins of the role models of your youth. Take a bird's-eye view of any given situation and analyze it—not as a victim, but rather as a student looking to move forward.

"You are what you eat."
—Every diet expert ever

I'm a big believer in watching what I consume, even as I sit here, with my probably-could-stand-to-lose-a-couple-of-pounds physique. (I do not subscribe to the must-have-abs-to-be-successful mantra.)

A lot of who you are is based on what you consume. Much like being careful to avoid labeling yourself or repeating patterns of negativity you were exposed to early in life, your daily diet matters.

Listen, I'll never write a diet book. I mean, I have my own approach to health, but it sure as hell doesn't merit 188 pages. It does, however, merit two pages, so let's talk about what I do and do not consume.

Let's say you start your day with two bowls of Cocoa Pebbles. Let's say your pantry is filled with Double Stuf Oreos, Lay's potato chips, the entire Little Debbie collection, and six twelve-packs of Cherry Coke. Let's say you eat Big Macs for lunch and fatty pork ribs and torpedo-sized baked potatoes for dinner. And let's say you finish off the night with two or three or seven beers. If you're putting all that garbage into your stomach, what kind of outcome can you expect? Will you be underweight or overweight?

Will your cholesterol be under 200 or over 450? Will you run a half-marathon, or run out of breath halfway up a flight of stairs?

If you're honest with yourself, the answers to those questions are obvious. If you're not honest with yourself and need visual proof that subsisting on sweet cereal, overly processed pastries, and fatty proteins isn't a wise idea—if you need some help realizing that this lifestyle could end in an early death—meet Morgan Spurlock.

In 2004, Spurlock decided to do an experiment: For one month, he'd eat nothing but McDonald's for breakfast, lunch, and dinner. And because Morgan is Morgan, he decided to document the entire adventure on film, which became a classic Oscar-nominated documentary called *Super Size Me*.

Spurlock knew that this batshit crazy diet would wreak havoc upon his body, but he wanted to prove a point, and man, did he prove it. Over his four weeks in eating hell, the then thirty-two-year-old gained almost twenty-five pounds—that's basically a pound a day, people—his cholesterol jumped 170 points, his liver looked as if he'd been a decades-long alcoholic, and he suffered from crippling headaches, scary mood swings, and erectile dysfunction.

Morgan proved that what you consume matters. My diet takes it a step further.

And my diet has nothing to do with food, and everything to do with content. It involves understanding what you're consuming and how the consumption makes you think and feel.

Many Drifters give as little thought to what they put into their brain as what they put in their mouth. Rather than, say, reading an amazing book designed to help you stop Drifting along, they will doomscroll and fill their heads with nonsense, negativity, jealousy, and disappointment. I challenge you to ask yourself how you feel after a thirty-minute TikTok binge. How much of what you saw made you mad? How much made you feel worse about your current situation? How much bummed you out? I would be willing to bet anything that the negativity far outweighed the joy.

If you find yourself addicted to fast foot or fast bandwidth, you might want to find somebody who can help you wean off this sort of crap.

And it's not just social media—it's all media. Back in my younger days when I was Drifting along, my favorite band in the world was Social Distortion. The lyrics to some of the songs that I would sing at the top of my lungs were so self-defeating that, in retrospect, it seems crazy. Today, I still love the band, but the things you repeat to yourself over and over have an effect on you. If you're screaming how much of a loser you are—even if it's to a killer soundtrack—it's going to have some consequences, even if you don't realize it at the time.

This isn't to say that, content-wise, you have to entirely deprive yourself. Go ahead and have a cheat day where you spend half an hour on Insta and an hour watching TikTok cat videos—but don't binge. Sure, hours and hours of lousy media and lousier lunches might feel comforting in the moment, but if you're Drifting, you don't need comfort. You need solutions.

And there aren't any solutions on Kim Kardashian's Twitter (or X) page.

Now I'm sure Social Distortion's front man, Mike Ness, doesn't care that his lyrics are on the depressing side—truth be told he's probably writing those songs for a target audience. And just like Social D's lyrics, what you say is going to attract or repel a certain audience, so mind what you say.

A few years back, one of my agents was quoted in a *Fortune* article about the Las Vegas real estate market, and that quote was incredibly pessimistic. I'm not saying she wasn't right—the market fluctuates on a regular basis, and sometimes pessimism is the present reality—but I will say that being Debbie Downer in a respected magazine with a huge circulation was a lousy idea. Honesty is sometimes most definitely not the best policy.

The impact of her interview was immediate and harsh.

The quote found its way onto social media, and much of her client base saw it, and many of them interpreted her thoughts as, *I don't believe in what I do. I'm telling you to buy a house, but deep down, I don't think you should.*

Nobody was surprised when her business crumbled. After all, who wants to work with somebody who doesn't stand behind their product—especially when that product can cost a buyer seven figures?

This was shortsighted thinking on her part; she was likely trying for clicks, and clicks don't pay the bills (unless they're on OnlyFans). While this message may have resonated in our echo chamber society with those who have no intention of buying a house at the moment, it alienated those that may have to buy one right now. She could have delivered the same message without pushing away a potential customer base simply by choosing better words.

Me, I would have said, "Look, the market conditions are definitely a turbulent sea right now, but if you have to sail into them, then I'm going to be the lighthouse for you guiding you as safely as possible."

See? I said the same thing she said about the market, without alienating my clients.

Words can repel.

Words can attract.

Words matter, whether they're spoken, or written, or tweeted.

You can speak/write/tweet logically or foolishly.

So be logical.

When somebody I'm mentoring needs to get into a positive mind state, I'll often give them my thoughts on mantras, because I can't discuss the concept of helping yourself without discussing helpful chanting.

See, I love mantras—love, love, love.

One of the first things I tell a mentee in my coaching program is, "Write down a list of all your limiting beliefs. Include why you're not where you want to be in your business life or your financial life. Include why you think you're too old to learn new things. Include why you think you don't have enough clients. And be brutally honest with me and with yourself."

After they complete their lists, I'll tell them, "Now write the exact opposite of all those things."

After completing that list, I'll tell them, "Congratulations, that list of opposites is now your daily mantra."

If you've never devised a mantra, no sweat. There's nothing to be intimidated about, because your mantra can be as black and white as, "I have an abundance of money. I have an abundance of clients. I learn new skills."

Once you lock down your mantra, write it on sticky notes and post them on your bathroom mirror, and make it the wallpaper on your phone, and iron it onto a T-shirt, then say it out loud, every single time you see it. Maybe in the morning, maybe in the evening, maybe when you brush your teeth, maybe when you get out of the shower, maybe all of the above—just say it and embrace it. (Even today—even though I've escaped The Drift time and again—I still get my mantra on... and no, I'm not telling you what it is. My mantra is my mantra, and your mantra should be your mantra.) See, your subconscious mind doesn't always know what's real and what isn't, so if you just start telling yourself a different story, well, it's like muscle memory. You'll start to believe it.

This isn't about manifesting. This isn't The Secret. This is about telling yourself a better story and convincing yourself to become a better version: You 2.0.

Eventually, your subconscious will start to believe it. And that's when the real fun begins. As you'll come to realize, talking to yourself is important...but not nearly as important as talking to others.

A lot of others.

It took me years to realize that one of the best ways to change your life is to surround yourself with better people—people you admire, people who work harder, people who have a great attitude, people who can both offer and accept aid in a graceful, useful manner.

But, John, you might be wondering, *how do I find these people, what with all the Drifting I'm dealing with?*

Damn good question.

One way to improve your tribe is to become a better resource, to become a Connector. And what better place to start than your phone?

Everybody who knows me knows I'm both a phone person and a people person, so I regularly get hit with something along the lines of, *Do you know somebody in* [this industry] *or* [this city] *or* [this company]*?*

I'm an obsessive contact-keeper, so anybody who I think can help me, or a friend, or a colleague, or a family member goes right into my phone. That way, when I get the make-me-an-introduction, I can say, "I'm going to connect you via three-way text to this dude, or that dude, or this other dude . . ."

Boom, connection made.

Maybe I don't personally get something out of it in the moment, but I helped somebody, and they might come back and help me, and if we help each other, we become friendly, and if we become friendly, we might realize that we want to be in one another's circle.

For instance, last week I was at a networking event where I was asked by a colleague, "Hey, John, do you know this guy?" He mentioned an unfamiliar name.

I said, "Never heard of him."

"Well, you should know him. You guys would get along great."

I never say no to a potential partner in crime, so I pulled him up on Instagram—we'll call him Caleb—and, sure enough, Caleb was already following me. So I followed Caleb back, then hit him up with a message: "I'm sitting here with Kenny Simpson, and he says we should connect."

Almost immediately, Caleb responded with a heart emoji. After some back-and-forth we scheduled to meet for lunch. Who knows if it'll amount to anything, but Kenny Simpson's a good guy, and Caleb might be a good guy. Worth it.

The point of all this is that sometimes you shouldn't wait for people to approach you or ask for a connection. If you see people in your network that could get together and do good stuff, connect them. Become the guy who's known as The Connector. It could lead to something great—and, if I'm being fully honest, I also recommend this because successful matchmaking feels pretty damn good.

When you're The Connector—when you're trying to be of value to your friends, family, and colleagues—you have to facilitate matchups with no regard for reciprocation. If you're doing something because you expect somebody to pay you back, that's horse trading. If you want this to work—if you want to create a better circle—don't horse trade. Be a go-giver, not a go-getter.

What you don't want to do is either ooze negativity or associate with negativity-oozers. Remember to be the lighthouse, because if you become known as the person with the black cloud over your head, nobody will want to be around you, nobody will want to work with you, and nobody will offer you their help. That said, we all sometimes find ourselves in a bad way, and we all need somebody to talk us off the ledge—but keep your negativity in the tightest part of your circle.

Conversely, if you demonstrate outward positivity, your inner negativity will drift away. And that particular kind of drift—the lowercase drift—is a beautiful thing.

CHAPTER 11

NETWORKING

YOU + THEM = AWESOMENESS

For aspiring entrepreneurs—hell, for established entrepreneurs as well—networking is key. Working the metaphorical room can build up your business foundation, or your staff, or your contacts list in the most efficient, most effective manner possible.

And I know this because, in my early years, I messed up my network situation. A lot.

Listen, if you're a bullheaded type, you might feel compelled to do everything yourself because you think you're smart, capable, and energetic enough to be Mr. or Ms. DIY—and I get that. Thing is, you *can't* do everything yourself. Connecting yourself to the world at large—especially the *business* world at large—gives you an advantage.

But you have to be meticulous about it.

Quick! Think of your favorite person... *You liar*... Your favorite person is you!

That's okay—my favorite person is me, too. (My family—parents, wife, kids, and even a few cousins—are a *very* close second.) That being the case, we tend to be attracted to folks who resemble our favorite person (us), and while the people in question may be similar to you in taste, style, sense of humor, and outlook on the world, it may not be the wisest idea to clog your network with mini-mes. It's great to have them as a dinner partner, but not necessarily as a work partner.

To wit, when I was in the bar business, I was always around bar people. When I was in the tech industry, I was always around tech people. That's what we do—we tend to surround ourselves with people with, more or less, the exact same skills as us. Makes sense, really—as long as you're in the same industry, you'll always have a connection with them.

My *Apprentice* stretch was the first time I was ever around a bunch of other people who were high-level performers from a variety of venues—and I dug it. I realized I could learn so much from successful experts outside of my field(s). It taught me that a diverse network is crucial, as a network filled with John Gaffords would lead to overlap and stagnation. (Sure, I'd love to watch a game with seven John Gaffords, but in terms of running my business, one John Gafford is plenty.)

How can incorporating diversity into your life help you out of The Drift? Well, we all look for comfort, ease, and the path of least resistance, which is why we gravitate toward rebooted versions of ourselves. At any of my service industry gigs, after everybody called it a night, we'd all go to a bar and discuss our service industry gig. Then we'd do it the next day, and the next, and the next; lather, rinse, repeat. And this wasn't always a good idea, because if you hang out with service industry lifers, you might think, *This gig is fine. I'm comfortable, my friends and colleagues are comfortable, so*

I'll put aside that business plan I've been working on and stay at this restaurant for a decade.

It became a cycle that was almost impossible to break, and it needed to be broken, because if you hang out with a bunch of broke people, you'll think that being broke is okay. If you hang out with five idiots, consider yourself idiot number six. If you hang out with a bunch of heavy people, you'll start to believe that living a healthy lifestyle is optional. If your friend's credit sucks, your Equifax score could plummet and you won't care, because if it's okay for your pal, it becomes okay for you.

So next time you're at a get-together, be it social or business, look around the room and ask yourself, *Do these people make me better? Do they challenge me? Do they bring something to the table other than a mutual love of reality television?*

If the answer to any of these questions is no, rethink your contacts.

See, being around the right people will both make you expect more from yourself and show you what's possible. So look at your contacts, figure out who helps make you the best you that you can be—and figure out who won't suck you into The Drift—then once you separate the goods from the bads, thin the herd and start deleting.

Thing is, your herd might be so lousy that you suddenly find yourself with a thumb-sized network. And thumb-sized doesn't get the job done. So how do you replenish?

Meetups.

What's a meetup? It's exactly what it sounds like. It's a meeting of random people all circled around a common theme. Could be real estate, could be crypto, could be anything.

But, John, you might be thinking, *where can I find a meetup in my area?*

Well, my friends, fortunately for all of us, there's a little thing called the Internet, where you can head over to Google and do a search on "Meetups" and "[Insert your home city here]." Hell, I just did that very search using "real estate" and "Las Vegas," and do you know how many hits there were? A whopping six hundred. So you have zero excuse for not utilizing this fantastic resource.

When you go to a meetup, you might feel out of place. You might be in a different age demographic than most of your fellow attendees. You might have a different level of success. You might be in a sector of your industry that doesn't jibe with anybody else in the room.

So. Fucking. What.

I'm often the oldest guy at these get-togethers, but I don't care. If somebody thirty years younger than me has a great approach to their business, I'm listening. I won't dismiss them due to an age difference, and if they're worth having in your network, neither will they.

Your meetup of choice doesn't have to be intimate. Thought leaders like Cody Sperber and Dan Fleyshman will often rent out ten-thousand-plus-seat venues for their events—and if there are ten thousand entrepreneurs with whom you can rub shoulders, chances are at least twenty of them will be network-worthy. (Side note: Following these experts on social media—LinkedIn, Instagram, and Twitter are my go-tos—will keep you in the loop regarding their events. And following John Gafford will keep you in the loop regarding my events.)

So if you say you can't find a meetup, you're not looking.

My buddy Ari Gold—and he's a real buddy, not the character from Entourage—is a younger guy from whom I've learned a whole bunch about networking on social media. When you hit up his Instagram, you'll see photos and/or videos of him playing beer pong with Post Malone or standing backstage with Ludacris. This guy knows everybody, so I had him on my podcast.

One of the first questions I asked was, "Ari, how do you get these celebrities in your circles? And how do you get into theirs?"

He said, "I don't ask them for shit. I never ask these guys for anything, ever. I'm the guy that brings value to them. They're always calling me, wanting me to hang out, wanting me to do this, wanting me to go here, wanting me to go there. But I never ask them for tickets or anything like that."

Much to his credit, Ari uses social media with positive intention. He doesn't post any nonsense, because he wants to be seen as a serious person, somebody who can be counted on. He won't post pictures of himself, say, guzzling a Guinness and falling off the side of a boat. Sure, that might be funny to him and his five closest friends, but the rest of the universe will be far from impressed. He knows that social media shouldn't be treated like a text chain where you share the kind of stupid shit you send your friends—stupid shit that can get you canceled.

Expert social media types never share anything that's unnecessary. Think about GaryVee, one of the savviest social media experts in history. He posts constantly on all social platforms, but what do we know about him? Not much. We know he loves the Jets. We know he collects Pokémon cards. We know he likes going to garage sales. Gary is always on brand, and because of it, he has arguably the biggest network in the business world.

Anyhow, the takeaway from all of this is that when you're building your network, don't ask, *What can I get out of this person?* Ask, *How can I bring value to this person?* That mindset will enable you to establish and maintain a relationship, which is key because being associated with successful people is going to rub off on you, is going to make you strive for more, is going to make you want to take yourself to another level.

This isn't to say that the relationship should be totally nonreciprocal. There might be a time you'll need something from them...but if you've already proven your value, they'll view collaborating with you as a win for them.

To that end, let's check in with one of the Gaffords who's way more talented than me, that being my sister Mandy.

Right now, Mandy hosts a massively popular talk radio show in Denver. She's so huge that she's able to book almost any guest she targets. When I started my podcast, I couldn't book anybody. But, because she's awesome, my sister was willing to help.

When I'd reach out to a potential guest for my show, I'd introduce myself, then say, "I know your time is incredibly valuable. I'd love to have you on my podcast. It's just kind of starting out. I don't know if I'm going to be able to move your needle, but if you do this, I've already got you set up to be on my sister's show, which has this giant reach, which will definitely move some needles for whatever you're trying to promote."

Did that work? Of course.

Every single time? Yes. Every single time.

Would they have said yes to me without the added bonus of an appearance on my sister's show? Highly unlikely.

All these years later, I'm on the opposite side of those requests. Whenever somebody asks me to appear on their pod, I'll think, *Time and energy are my most valuable resources, so is this worth my time? Does this add value to my business or personal life?*

So I'll ask the booker, "What's your show's reach? What're the demographics? Do you know which industries your listeners come from?"

This may seem like bad karma—after all, I was once in a position where I was the supplicant answering those questions, and giving mediocre answers at that—but this makes sense for everybody. If it's a waste of my time, it's probably a waste of the host's time...and that's time that they can use to tighten up their network.

I like to hear myself talk. You like to hear yourself talk. Everybody likes to hear themselves talk. And what better place to talk than on a podcast?

Given that my podcast has developed a loyal, targeted audience—and given that, as noted, we all like to yammer on and on about ourselves—it's now relatively easy for me to book quality guests.

Some of my guests are friends or business colleagues, while others are people I've never met in my life but *want* to meet because I think they bring something to the table. And if they do indeed bring something to the table—and if they have a good time on the show—well, there's somebody I can add to my network.

Now, admittedly, podcasting isn't for everybody—if you're Drifting, there's a fair chance you don't have the means or wherewithal to start your own show. And while this isn't a pod book, here're a few things I've learned in my brief time as a broadcaster.

USE YOUR CONTENT OVER AND OVER AGAIN

If you have a one-hour show, you can cut that into twenty-five or thirty quickie clips to post on your social media. Make sure you link all the postings to the pod's home page, whether that's on your own site or Spotify.

STAY FOCUSED DURING INTERVIEWS

You always want your listeners thinking about what you want them to think about. If it's a real estate show, don't spend half an hour discussing college football.

HAVE A GOAL

If your goal is to grow your listener base, throw some money at a publicist who's proven successful at getting ears. If you want to grow your network, book guests you want in your network. If you want to appeal to Realtors, talk the Realtor language.

BE INTERESTED

Ask pointed questions, then really listen to the answer. If you don't stay in the moment—if you're thinking about your next question, or what you're having for lunch after the show—you'll lose both your guest and the audience. If you pay attention, your guest will have a great time, you'll have a great conversation, and your network will have grown.

BE FLEXIBLE

You may have prepared what you believe to be ten perfect questions, but if the conversation veers into different territory—and that territory is interesting to you—roll with it. Because if it's interesting to you, it'll probably be interesting to your audience.

DON'T BE INTIMIDATED BY THE PROCESS

Quality podcasting gear isn't too expensive, getting the show distributed is simple, navigating your way through audio software isn't as daunting as it seems, and after some practice, hosting a show will become second nature. You can't let fear hold you back, as that's super-Drifty behavior.

In summary, I have found there is no better way to connect with someone and add them into my network than by sitting with them one-on-one for an hour and talking about their favorite subject: themselves.

But if you want to grow your network faster, you need more than one-on-ones; you need some big, curated rooms.

> "No mind is complete by itself. It needs contact and association with other minds to grow and expand."
>
> —Napoleon Hill, author of *Think and Grow Rich*

If the meetups we discussed earlier are level one of growing your network, mastermind groups are level ten. The right mastermind group is designed to do one thing for you: collapse time. Being around a bunch of people who basically do the same thing as you—and are doing it at a high level—gives you an unlimited resource pool to dip into, a pool that can help you solve any problem you may have at lightning speed.

How much do I believe in these things? I spend over six figures a year on mastermind groups, enough for a down payment on a great house. That's how important these groups are to me.

For those of you who don't spend six figures on mastermind groups—hell, for those of you who spend *zero* figures on mastermind groups—here's what you're missing, according to the concept's inventor, the abovementioned Napoleon Hill: "The coordination of knowledge and effort between two or more people who work towards a definite purpose in a spirit of harmony. No two minds ever come together without creating a third, invisible, intangible force, which may be linked to a [mastermind]."

Good stuff, right? It becomes even more impressive when you learn that Hill wrote this in 1937.

Fortunately, my six-figure mastermind expenditure has paid off in spades—but it didn't pay off right away, because I didn't know how to properly utilize the format. I didn't realize that for one of these groups to work for you, you need to find a tribe with whom you jibe. Like if you're a Realtor, you can't arbitrarily join a group that focuses on real estate, because "real estate" can mean fifty different things. Track down the *right* real estate group for *you*.

I've embraced the concept so much that I started up my own group, one called Broker Click, a group I designed for high performing real estate brokers. It's a huge expenditure—putting together the video invitations, for example, cost $15,000—but I was willing to spend that kind of money in order to assure that I delivered a great event. I sent these magical video invitations out almost in unison, during a stretch when interest rates were through the roof and every big broker in America was freaking out at least a little bit. Like I said before, if I can't do it right, I'm not gonna do it at all, and with response cooling with the market, I decided to cancel my event.

As you read this, you might think I look at this as a failure. *Wrong*. You see, I was able to turn it into a profitable win. How? Well, I contacted my good friend Kent Clothier, who runs the Boardroom mastermind for real estate, and asked him if I could fold my newfound tribe into his existing one, after which he would simply pay me a referral for each member who joined Boardroom. Success—I recouped my entire investment, plus he and I still got to network with these awesome brokers that I recruited across the country.

That's a win. And a big one at that.

I should point out that if you want to start your own mastermind group—which is a terrific idea if you want to ramp up your contact list and begin your trip out of The Drift—you don't need to invest $100,000, or have another mastermind to fold into as a safety net. Hell, you don't need to invest $200. Just post the event on your LinkedIn page or in a targeted Facebook group, then send Evites out to your friends. There's no need to rent a venue; the group can meet at a local dive bar. As long as you get the right people in the right room, your event will be a success.

At the event, make certain you're *present*.

Don't just walk around and ask a generic question like, "What do you do?" You see, at events like this, it's key to be memorable, and you can do just that by doing the unexpected.

I do this by saying, "Tell me about you."

Simple, right?

When they start on their oft-repeated thirty-second elevator pitch about their position or their company, I stop them and say, "No, I don't want to know about what you do. I want to know about *you*. Where are you from? Are you married? Do you have kids?"

Do this, and you'll see their demeanor change before your eyes.

If you discuss hobbies, mutual interests, and families, the attendees will walk away thinking, *Huh, that John Gafford doesn't want to just exchange business cards. He wants to learn about me as a human being. I'm comfortable hanging out with him, so I'll be comfortable doing business with him.*

This is how I become memorable.

One thing you *don't* want to do at your mastermind meeting—or at *any* mastermind meeting, for that matter—is spout off. This isn't to say you can't offer an opinion, but do so in a mature, subtle manner. See, within a large group, there are often fragmented groups, and the fragmented group might have a different view of life than the majority of the attendees. So if somebody asks, "What're your thoughts on how the [insert a political party] is approaching the economy?" answer with a nonanswer.

One of the surest ways to alienate somebody at this sort of event is to loudly proclaim a controversial opinion about a hot-button topic. If somebody throws this sort of question at me, I'll generally say something along the lines of, "I don't have an opinion on that." That way, nobody is offended, and you won't come off as a contradictory asshole.

Because nobody wants to have a contradictory asshole in their network. Nobody.

This is gonna sound like the dumbest thing in the world—certainly the dumbest thing you'd ever read in a self-help book—but some of you out there need to hear this.

Be nice.

You never know who you're talking to. You never know who they are today, and you never know who'll they'll be ten years from now, so kindness is a must.

For instance, I've always gone out of my way to be nice to musicians. (As a musician myself, I know that a little bit of kindness and respect goes a long way.) And my kindness has nothing to do with whether the musician in question had a gold record and a tour bus, or a twelve-pack of beer and a shitty van. I respect them all because they've worked hard to hone their craft, and they're doing what they do because they love it.

Because of my sincere approach to "band peeps," I've been able to establish and maintain relationships with artists who, when I first met them, were scuffling, then went on to become huge. For example, I used to book a few members of the Zac Brown Band, including Zac himself, who used to play guitar for $100 a night on the patio of one of my bars, because that's all we could afford to pay him. Because I was good to them before they blew up, I consider them friends.

The list of guys I met back in the day who've since blown up is long and fulfilling. Hell, I met my wife because I was screwing around while out on tour living the rock and roll life. But that's a tale for another book.

It's also key to be nice to everyone who is *not* there. One of the biggest faux pas of my networking life happened at a Dallas real estate mastermind called "The Avengers." I had met this guy at the bar that I really liked, and a group of us were swapping stories. I happened to bring up Cobalt Lounge and jokingly said, "Yeah, it was great until Ray Lewis came in and people got murdered." The conversation carried on about world domination in the real estate market until our group split off to chat up others. At these events, Instagram is often the business card of choice, and once back at my room, I realized I had forgotten to connect with the dude I thought was cool. So I pulled up his IG to follow him.

And there it was: At least three photos in his grid of him with Ray Lewis. Not meet-and-greet photos, mind you, but we-hang-out-all-the-time photos.

Ouch. Foot in mouth. Connection lost. All because I said something that wasn't nice.

So. Just. Be. Nice.

If you take that approach to your business life, you're on your way to an all-expenses paid trip out of The Drift—but this isn't a quick process. Even if you put everything you've read in this chapter into action *right this second*, you won't have a notable network for months. Networking isn't just about exchanging email addresses. It's about making sincere connections, and that sort of connection requires patience and a big-picture view.

You need to look at your potential network as a collection of dots that you can selflessly connect without expectations. Make a connection so you can help somebody else make a connection. As an example, check out this near-perfect text chain:

> Them: "John, do you know anybody at [such-and-such company]?"
>
> Me: "I do. You want me to put you in touch?"

Them: “Please, that would be great.”

Me: “Cool. Done.”

Man, little makes me happier in life than connecting those dots, because those dots bring me one step closer to having my own GaryVee-sized network.

CHAPTER 12

STAYING CENTERED

DON'T BE AN EGO ID . . . IOT

Let's talk egos.

Sometimes egos are useful, while in other instances, they royally screw us up—and the screwups come to pass when you allow your ego to work against you.

My friend Kevin Griffin—amazing songwriter and lead singer of Better Than Ezra—wrote a wonderful book called *The Greatest Song*. In it, he dropped the theory that *your ego is not your amigo*, and you must understand that it's often not in lockstep with the rest of your psyche.

To wit: There're movies you don't like, there're bands you don't dig, there're restaurants you don't care for, and you can't really put your finger on why. You can't give a specific reason—all you know is that they're just not for you.

And it works both ways. Not everybody is going to like you.

To elaborate, I'll point you to a book called *The Four Agreements: A Practical Guide to Personal Freedom* by Don Miguel Ruiz, and those agreements of Don Miguel are something else:

- Be impeccable with your word.
- Don't take anything personally.
- Don't make assumptions.
- Always do your best.

Great stuff, and I could chop it up about this all day, but for the sake of this ego discussion, let's focus on number two.

You may think you're the best person on the planet and everybody should love you—but you're wrong for two reasons:

1. My wife is the best person on the planet.
2. Jesus didn't get them all, so what makes you think you can?

Understanding and accepting that you're not everybody's cup of tea is one of the first things you need to do if you want to sublimate that ego of yours and keep yourself balanced—and balance is crucial, because imbalance can destroy a relationship, and little in your business life is more important than your relationships. (Hell, little in your *personal* life is more important than your relationships.)

A huge component of staying centered and keeping your ego in check is realizing and accepting that *not everything is about you*. If a colleague is short and snappy with you, there's a fair chance that their lousy mood is due to some external factor that has absolutely zero to do with you, and everything to do with the fact that the colleague in question spilled piping hot coffee on their lap and singed a part of their body that nobody wants singed.

Even as a business owner who's jumped plenty of hurdles to get where I am, it's something I constantly battle with, especially when dealing with an upset customer. When faced with anger, you feel slighted and your ego tells you, *How dare this person speak to me in that manner! I'm me, and I don't deserve to be treated that way.*

At that point, you need to tell your ego to chill the fuck out. Figure out the customer's issue, and remain polite, and thoughtfully communicate, because more often than not, their anger stems from factors that have nothing to do with you.

Don't get me wrong: This isn't an easy mindset. In the face of an angry client, of course you'll get defensive, especially if you've done everything you can to please said client.

It's like this with any conflict. You have to remember you're not the main character in their story—you're just a bit player. Keeping this at the front of your mind is an easy way to avoid serious ego damage.

It's equally crucial to keep your ego from getting inflated—and in this day and age of social media, man, it can get inflated fast. Conversely, just as fast as the old ego balloon gets filled, social media can pop it.

To illustrate, let's revisit those mastermind groups.

At one of my early groups, I was told by a colleague of a colleague of a colleague, "John, you've got to boost engagement on social media. That's what'll take your business to the next level. And if you don't, well, you'll miss out on a whole lot of business."

The Gafford Ego thought, *I'm crushing it on social. These guys can't tell me what to do.* But after deep dives into my unimpressive Instagram engagement metrics, I thought, *Huh, these guys might be right*, so I set aside my ego and hired an outside company to ramp up my socials.

The company got my IG follower count up to 120,000—what an ego boost! But soon, my new grandiose stature came back down to earth. It quickly became apparent that these 120,000 people weren't *my* people; they were followers who were bought and paid for. The numbers were great. The engagement wasn't. (Turns out IG doesn't like high follower counts and low engagement. They think you've artificially inflated your numbers with bots or bot-like schemes. Which you probably have.)

When the follower count grew to 120,000, I realized it had nothing to do with me or my business, and that bruised my little feelings. Which was stupid.

The story has a happy ending, though: I've eliminated the bots, and now my followers are actual followers who engage and appreciate. My ego now appreciates the lower number because it realizes that the size is way less important than the quality. It's better for business when your people are on your frequency.

So, y'know, don't buy bots. It's bad for your mental health.

Don't get me wrong: You *have* to have a healthy ego. Too much humility chips away at your confidence. Like if Kobe Bryant or Michael Jordan were overly humble they wouldn't have been the leaders they were. Sure, Kobe sometimes deferred to O'Neal, and MJ sometimes deferred to Pippen, but when there was twenty seconds left in the game and the Lakers or Bulls were down by a point, the alpha was taking the final shot, Shaq or Scottie be damned.

So you have to find that balance. You have to figure out how to keep your ego in check...but not too much. And that balance is really hard to strike. It takes time and effort. But you can do it.

If you realize you need to change how you interact with clients, *change how you interact with your clients*. If you realize you need to change the way you present yourself to the world, *change the way you present yourself to the world*. If you realize you need to entirely reinvent yourself, *entirely reinvent yourself*. Don't let that ego of yours keep you Drifting. You can become unstuck if you put in the effort.

Once again, let's take a visit to the networking world.

At some of these meetings, your fellow attendees will equate you with your bank account—for example, *Hey, that Gafford dude is an okay guy, I guess, but I read that he just wrapped up this lucrative deal, so I'm going to kiss his ass like it's never been kissed before.*

(Egos, it must be noted, love to have their asses kissed.)

This sort of interaction is a waste of time and energy for everybody involved. It's a waste for me because being told how awesome I am by somebody who doesn't think that I actually am awesome is foolish. And accepting and believing empty praise is equally inane—especially when you have to go to the front of the room and give a lecture.

When you're speaking at a networking event, you don't have an O'Neal or a Pippen to whom you can defer—it's all you. And if you take a puffed-up ego to the lectern—if you think, *I'm the man, I'm the dude, I'm the guy*—you've lost all authenticity. Even though a handful of folks listening to your talk were kissing your ass thirty minutes ago, they'll recognize any insincerity. That doesn't mean they'll stop kissing your ass, but said kissing will become even more contrived, which keeps the vicious cycle going and going and going.

Early in my career, my ego issue was muddied by the fact that I was terrified to stand in front of a room of high-level performers. Even though I had a high opinion of myself, there was a part of me that thought, *I'm going to shit the bed, and these people who think I'm so awesome will see the man behind the curtain pulling the levers, and they ain't gonna like him.*

Eventually I centered myself and found a sweet spot between confidence and humility. When you're honest with your associates—and when you're honest with yourself—you can grow not just in business, but also as a person.

Remember that scene in *Ted Lasso* when Ted and Rupert Mannion got into a high-stakes darts match? At the climax, Ted dropped a monologue in which he discussed the importance of curiosity: "Guys have underestimated me my entire life, and for years, I never understood why. It used to really bother me. Then one day I was driving my little boy to school, and I saw this quote by Walt Whitman. It was painted on the wall there and it said, 'Be curious, not judgmental.' I like that."

I like that, too, because it hammers home the point that if you don't challenge yourself, if you don't take in new information on a regular basis, it becomes impossible to remain centered and to grow. In other words, if your ego tells you, *You're fine as you are*, you're toast.

To illustrate, let's talk surfing.

I'm the worst surfer in the world. I almost drown half the time I hit the waves, and both my ego and my body always take a beating, but I don't give a shit because I *love* it. Note: I didn't start surfing until I was fifty, in part because I was worried about looking foolish in front of a bunch of strangers who A) I'll never see again, and B) Don't give a fuck what kind of surfer I am. But once I got out of my own way—once I realized that curiosity was far more important than being judged—it was game on.

I continued to challenge myself.

I continued to take in new information.

I continued to be curious.

I continued to stop worrying about being judged.

I'm still not an expert wave-rider, but I don't care. I adore it, and it keeps my brain and body growing and evolving, even when I take a waterlogged face-plant.

We talked about checking your ego; now let's talk about staying centered.

One of the biggest mistakes I see people make in this area is that they become what they do. And because what you do will probably change several times throughout your life—either voluntarily or involuntarily—this is a really good way to set yourself up for failure.

When I was running Cobalt, *Esquire* ranked us as the best nightclub on the East Coast. It was a nonstop party before the article hit, but once word got out, every celebrity in the world rolled through that door. Thanks to our visible success, I became a local celebrity of sorts. I stopped being John Gafford and became John from Cobalt. (Or, as it was often said, John Fromcobalt.)

When the club closed and I lost the gig, I also lost my identity. And losing your identity—and not being able to recover it—can lead to a lengthy Drift appearance.

Not too long thereafter, a new club opened in Midtown Atlanta called Lava Lounge. I went on opening night, and the line was wrapped around the planet, but I wove through the crowd, walked right up to the front, and said to the door guy—whom I'd never met—"Hey, man, what's up?"

He gave me a skeptical once-over and grunted, "What?"

Elaborating, I said, "I'm John Fromcobalt."

He said, "Cobalt closed three months ago. Get to the back of the line."

Shit. I went from running the best club on the East Coast to being sent to the back of the line. As stupid as this example seems now, my twenty-seven-year-old ego was shattered. I had let my entire identity get wrapped up in a job I didn't even control.

Two-plus decades and a lifetime of experience later, I'd never let anything that trivial upset me. I mean, I've got three very large businesses now that I love, but I could sell them tomorrow and it wouldn't bother me, as my identity is not wrapped up in the success of those companies. My identity now is husband, father, good dude.

But I had to figure that out for myself. I had to spend years calibrating my ego, years mapping out how to get and stay centered. The process would've been sped up considerably had somebody taken me aside and said, "John, you're not your job; you are not what you do. You're just you, and just being you is good enough." All in all, I'd have been better off.

Then again, I was twenty-seven, and twenty-seven-year-old males, generally speaking, have Drift-ian tendencies, and thus don't listen to that kind of advice, so that discussion might have ended abruptly, and the advice might have gone unheeded.

When you picked up this book, your first thought was undoubtedly, *I can't wait to get to the part where John talks about stoicism!*

Wait no longer, because it's stoic time... but before we dive in, we need to break down the concept of memento mori.

Memento mori is a Latin phrase that loosely translates to, "Remember you must die." Socrates expounded on it when he said, "[Philosophy is] about nothing else but dying or being dead."

How does this relate to ego? How does this relate to staying centered? How does this relate to moving past The Drift? Just stick with me here.

My friend Dan Fleyshman—who's an awesome, incredible entrepreneur—is a professional-level poker player. He once explained his success with the cards to me.

"If I have pocket aces and you have pocket kings and you flop the third king and crack my aces on the poker table and I lose a big pot, my blood pressure does not change. And the reason it doesn't change is because I understand that sometimes that's supposed to happen. It doesn't happen that often, but sometimes it's supposed to happen. So the key to it is understanding what could happen so you're never surprised by anything."

Talk about being stoic.

It's clear how Dan's approach to poker can parallel one's professional and personal life. People will leave, people will quit, people will break up with you, friends will float away, business deals will go bad, you will get fired. This all happens, and none of it is ideal, but this is when you consider another tenet of stoicism: amor fati.

Amor fati, which was introduced to the world by Friedrich Nietzsche, is the concept that we have to accept everything that happens to us, whether it's a gain or a loss, whether it's suffering or happiness, whether it's simple or difficult. Regardless of what's making you happy or sad, you have to embrace it with willpower, discipline, and consideration.

So there are your stoic bookends: Live your best life, but remember your life is finite. Taking that to heart is *literally* staying centered.

Listen, when you lose your job, you'll likely (and justifiably) be devastated. If the economy falls into the shitter, you might think that your life will soon follow. But, to quote a modern philosopher by the name of Taylor Swift, "Shake it off, shake it off, whoo-hoo-hoo."

Sure, it's easy for me, a relatively successful businessman, to sit here and say, "I know you're out of work, and I know your bank account is dwindling, and I know your ego is shattered, and I know you're as centered as 'free Britney Spears,' but it'll all be fine." But you know what? I was there. I was out of work. I had miniscule funds. I was ready to dance around on IG with knives. But I shook it off, and I sublimated my ego, and I paid attention to people who knew better than me, and I kept educating myself, and eventually—*eventually*—I managed to claw my way out of The Drift.

It wasn't easy. But you know what? It's not *supposed* to be easy.

Remember the last time you lost your car keys? Remember how you tore your house apart looking for them? Remember how you went on a stomach-destroying ice cream bender after you couldn't find them?

Not only was it within your powers to alleviate the issue, but you also have the tools to modify your reaction. In terms of the keys themselves, the solution is simple: *Make sure you have another set of keys*. By not having duplicates, you've created a single point of failure for yourself. When you turn that single point into multiple points, you significantly diminish your chance at an epic fail. In terms of the reaction, that's easy: Go to your 4-7-8 breathing method and stop buying six pints of Chubby Hubby.

I take the single-point-of-failure thing to heart when I'm onboarding new employees. Rather than throwing everybody into the deep end, I cross-train multiple employees on every single aspect of our business so there are at least three people who can handle any given task. And when somebody asks me, "Isn't this overkill?" I say, "No. Because what if somebody on my team gets eaten by a hippo?"

The single point of failure is eliminated, and thus nobody at my office has to be concerned about semiaquatic mammal attacks.

As I've made abundantly clear, I'm careful when it comes to the people I surround myself with. But choosing those friends, colleagues, and associates isn't always an identical process. Your current life circumstances will help you make those decisions—or the circumstances might even make those decisions for you.

Nobody wants to hear this, but there are points in life when you should leave some of your people behind. If they're dragging you down—if they're an anchor—you have to cut them loose. It doesn't matter how prestigious they are, or how wealthy they are, or how accomplished they are—if the person in question doesn't make you feel good about yourself, your life, or your business, they've gotta go, discussion over.

And that goes for you, too. Sometimes you might have to let yourself go . . . or at least the lesser version of yourself.

Out-of-control ego can turn you into your own anchor. Let me rephrase that: *My* out-of-control ego once turned *me* into an anchor. And it didn't involve a boat—for that matter, it involved the *opposite* of a boat, a mode of transportation that wasn't water-based, but rather sky-based.

When my bank account hit a certain point, one of my partners and I decided to buy ourselves a private jet. Why? Well, we figured it would be good for business, plus it would allow us to fly up to wine country for the weekend whenever we wanted.

We purchased a Dassault Falcon 50, and nobody was impressed. We looked not so much like serious businessmen, but rather like rich kids flaunting their wealth. Posting PJ photos on IG is all fine and good for twenty-three-year-olds. If you're fifty-plus, not so much.

It was a tone-deaf move, because my personal brand was "The Broker of the People." I was the guy fighting for his clients and agents everywhere, the guy in the foxhole who'd close any and every deal—and that's *not* the sort of guy who flaunts his airplane on social. Once I realized that the jet wasn't earning me any money, and it was making me look like a douchebag—once I realized it was a very, very expensive anchor—I sold it. Quickly.

You can't stay centered if you don't know how to read a room, if you don't understand to whom you're speaking, and if you can't figure out what they hope to hear or see. And I'm now painfully aware that potential property owners don't want to hear or see anything from a guy who pissed away his money on something so self-indulgent and show-offy as a plane.

If you have an opportunity to buy a private jet, just don't. It's an anchor, so buy a damn car.

I've spent years trying to balance my ego, and if I were writing this chapter in, say, 2013, it would've been about 621 pages long. As I write this, I'm happy to keep it succinct and to the point because, as noted, size doesn't matter, but quality does. And I'll wrap it up with what I hope is some short, sweet, and I believe hugely consequential advice.

Back in 2019, I went to an event called "Thrive: Making Money Matter," hosted by an entrepreneur named Cole Hatter. Cole was (and is) very big on having purpose-driven businesses, ones that don't just turn a profit, but mean something, that have intent.

That concept was a new one. For me, business had become about three things:

1. Making money.
2. Making money.
3. Making money.

What I didn't realize is that business should also be about giving back.

Simply put, a purpose-driven business has a built-in charitable component. In my case, for every deal we close, we make a donation to charities that mean something to us. In 2023, we bought something like 240,000 meals for a local food repository. Recently, a friend of mine named John Hopkins—from the Zac Brown Band—was diagnosed with ALS, so now all of our donations go to his ALS research foundation called Hop On a Cure.

If there's a better way to keep yourself centered—if there's a better way to keep your ego in check—I defy you to tell me what it is.

CHAPTER 13

RESILIENCE

THE BEAUTY OF BOUNCING BACK

The majority of the precepts in this book can be applied to any industry: everything from real estate, to minor league baseball, to health care, to carpet cleaning.

Carpet cleaning?

Yep. Carpet cleaning.

One of my colleague's colleagues—we'll call him Abbott—was a business coach, and he took on a client—we'll call him Costello—who was starting up a carpet cleaning company.

Abbott coached Costello for about six months, at which point Costello told Abbott, "I want to pivot away from this."

A surprised Abbott asked, "Um, why?"

Costello said, "I just don't think I'm ever going to get rich with carpet cleaning."

Abbott said, "Let me ask you this, Costello: Are there any multimillionaires who own carpet cleaning businesses?"

Costello said, "Dunno. I'm sure there are somewhere."

Abbott said, "That tells me carpet cleaning is not a bad business. That also tells me you're a shitty businessman."

Ouch. Cold. But probably true.

Unless you have an absurd infusion of cash into your bank account, six months isn't enough time to know whether your business will or won't work. During those six months, you might get knocked on your ass day after day after day, but the primary way your business will thrive—or even survive—will be for you to keep getting up day after day after day.

Many new entrepreneurs are fantastic at making excuses for failure. They blame the marketing plan, or the strategy, or the concept, or the staff, or the economy, or the location, or oversaturation, or any number of factors that might or might not be legit.

But the one thing they rarely blame is themselves.

I get it. Taking responsibility can be scary, especially after months and/or years of Drifting. But if you have an unwavering belief in yourself and a killer work ethic, you can be resilient enough to look in the mirror and figure out what you can do to save the shop.

In the early 1970s, instant karma was gonna getcha.

Today, it's instant gratification.

The Internet has conditioned us to expect *immediacy*. For instance, how pissed off do you get when ESPN.com takes thirty seconds to load, rather than the usual fifteen? The answer: *very*. Which is absurd.

Or try explaining to a five-year-old that when you were a kid, you had to wait until Saturday morning to watch your favorite cartoon—and you could only watch one episode at a time, because bingeing wasn't a thing.

Or think about how, thanks to the Amazons of the world, you can have a specialized, hard-to-find toothbrush on your doorstep less than twenty-four hours after you place your order.

And please don't get me started on third-party food delivery services.

This kind of consistent immediacy—the instant gratifying of America, if you will—hasn't done wonders for the concept of resilience. Since we've grown accustomed to getting goods and services so easily and so quickly, we've come to expect *everything* to happen quickly, and when it doesn't—when real life gets in the way—we're knocked for a loop. And since our psyches have been softened, it's harder to get back up.

On the other hand, believe it or not, you can be *too* resilient. You can take falling-and-getting-up too far. You can put yourself on the edge of being out of control. You can start to believe that you can get out of any situation intact.

Been there. Done that. Doesn't work.

After Cobalt went belly-up, I thought that I could still be the guy who did whatever he wanted, whenever he wanted, because I'd bounced back before, and I knew I could bounce back again...and quickly.

Wrong.

I blew through all my money, and when I say all my money, I mean *all of it*. I went from picking up checks at high-end restaurants to eating pouches of ramen.

Had I taken a beat, I might've realized that this particular down-and-out situation wasn't the same as any previous down-and-out situation I'd experienced, that things were more dire than I admitted to myself. I needed to rethink my approach to life.

I had to be *realistically* resilient.

Realistic resilience means understanding the negative consequences that can happen to you if you don't address your problems. It's not just about a blind faith—you can't walk around with your head Drifting in the clouds, trying to manifest success. It's about understanding consequences. Pushing forward is all fine and good, but don't take it to the point where you're falling into the abyss.

Bad stuff has happened.

Bad stuff is happening.

Bad stuff will happen.

I know, I know, this isn't what you want to read in a book that's supposed to be all about helping, but reality is reality, and reality isn't always optimal. But when reality bites you in the ass—and it will, sometimes in the good times, and sometimes in the bad—there's one thing you can do that can nudge you down a non-Drifty path . . .

Pause.

In this instance, *pause* doesn't mean *stop*. You can't get past the tough times by locking yourself in your apartment and binge-watching *Ozark*. No, I mean a mental pause, an emotional pause.

You can't beat down the uncontrollable external forces that put you in this position—fixing the economy, for instance, is well beyond our respective reach—but you can control how you react to the situation.

To that end, I share this parable:

> It's 1940 and over in Europe, World War II rages. But at a Nebraska farm, all is peaceful. As the sun rises, Farmer Bill milks his cows, and feeds his chickens, and does all the farm stuff he does every Monday morning. While he looks at his field of cornstalks, his neighbor sidles up to him and says, "Farmer Bill, your farm is looking better than ever."

Farmer Bill nods and says, "Maybe it is, maybe it isn't. We'll just have to see."

The next morning, five wild horses wander onto Farmer Bill's grounds. The neighbor notices, jogs over, and tells Farmer Bill, "Wow, look at all these horses! And they're all yours! And it didn't cost you a cent! Things must be the best they've ever been for you!"

Farmer Bill nods and says, "Maybe they are, maybe they aren't. We'll just have to see."

The following morning, Farmer Bill's son Tim saddles up one of the horses and jumps onto the animal's back. Being wild, the horse immediately bucks him off. Tim's leg is broken. He'll have a cast on it for at least two months, and after the cast comes off, he'll need surgery.

Upon hearing the news, the neighbor runs over and tells Farmer Bill, "I'm so sorry. This is terrible."

Farmer Bill nods and says, "Maybe it is, maybe it isn't. We'll just have to see."

The following morning, the neighbor comes to Farmer Bill's doorstep holding a letter. "This was mistakenly delivered to me."

Farmer Bill peers at the envelope—it's from the local army recruiter. He opens the letter and gives it a read: The recruiter is requesting Tim's presence at the local military base so he can begin training. Immediately.

The neighbor says, "What with his leg, Tim can't go to war, can he?"

Farmer Bill says, "No. He can't. And that's why I believe that no matter what, we always just have to see."

Farmer Bill didn't get too high. Farmer Bill didn't get too low. When things at the farm were good, Farmer Bill was steady. When faced with a difficult situation, Farmer Bill was steady. Because Farmer Bill was a realist. He knew bad stuff has happened, is happening, and will happen.

Farmer Bill took a pause.

This isn't to say that breaking your leg is a good thing; but it is to say that when you break your leg—be it a metaphorical leg or your actual limb—don't assume you're down for the count. Don't assume your hopes and dreams are out the window.

Don't Drift.

Sometimes speed is necessary. Sometimes you're so deep in The Drift that changes need to be made quickly. Sometimes a deadline eliminates the luxury of time.

But sometimes you need to ignore Andretti and pump the brakes, because if you're going to set out, you have to keep your eye on the destination, especially if the road is bumpy.

And believe me, in the wild, wacky world of real estate, the waters are *always* choppy.

Housing inventory fluctuates wildly. The rising and falling interest rates are jarring. The needs and wants of our clients are always changing. Our agents come and our agents go. Shit, as they say time and again, happens.

In the face of all this instability, resilience isn't about bouncing back, per se, but rather understanding what *is* working, what *isn't* working, what *might* work, what *might not* work, and what *won't* work.

Sometimes it's not necessary to focus on bouncing back. Sometimes, you just need to pivot.

Fortunately for me, my industry doesn't just allow for pivoting—it embraces it. You can prospect for new leads in original, innovative ways. You can tweak your marketing plans because they're never set in stone. You can take a new approach to your social media. You can start a podcast. You can create a mastermind meetup. You can make two hundred more sales calls each day. Don't quit until you have something on which to hang your hat. Fall in love with the process.

Speed up when you need to speed up. Slow down when you need to slow down. Control what you can control.

And get the fuck out of The Drift.

CHAPTER 14

CONCLUSION

Here we are, two hundred–ish pages later, and you have the tools…or at least you have *my* tools.

I know some of my tools aren't the kind of tools you asked for, or expected. Most of them are razor-sharp and, at some point, they will cause you pain. But even though my hammers, crowbars, and chisels will scrape your arms and legs, they'll also help you eliminate Drifting.

So what happens next? What do you do with the tools? Now that you realize it's okay to ask for help, and you understand that being a procrastinator is flat-out idiotic, and you accept that there's a time and place to take big swings, and you get that you don't need your negative past to screw up your positive present, ask yourself, *What's my next move?*

Simple:

You get earthbound.

You stay earthbound.

You move forward.

You bravely take a path you might not have otherwise taken.

You set your kids on the right path.

You beat the hell out of your friends and family at Monopoly.

You burst into Mark Burnett's office and tell him that if he doesn't cast you in his next show, he's a moron.

You quit Drifting and plant those feet of yours firmly on the ground.

You win.

And you keep winning.

ACKNOWLEDGMENTS

Man, am I glad you're reading this, and I have something for you at the end of this section. First, I have to thank some people.

Most importantly, I want to thank my wife, Gidget. You believed in me when I was still somewhere between "a work in progress" and "a lottery ticket." You've been my ride-or-die, my editor-in-chief of reality, the anchor that kept me from Drifting, and the sail that gets me where I want to go.

To my kids, Hayden and Roma—you motivate me daily to be the best version of myself. Everything I build, I build with you in mind. You're my legacy in motion.

Special shout-out to Jeff, the AM room service manager at the Ramada Inn on North Monroe Street in Tallahassee, Florida, and to Donald J. Trump, forty-seventh president of the United States. You two hold the distinct honor of being the only people to ever officially fire me. Honestly, more probably should've. That puts you two in a rare space; you should start a club.

To every guest who's ever sat across from me on *Escaping the Drift*: Thank you for bringing your wisdom, stories, scars, and hard-won truths. I've learned something from every single one of you—and if you've ever wondered if it made a difference, it did, not just in our listeners, but in me.

To all the agents, escrow officers, mortgage lenders, and support staff that choose to make our companies home, seeing your careers flourish under our flags gives me more pride than you will ever know.

To my friends and supporters—you know who you are. You've had my back when I was winning and when I was just winging it. I'm beyond grateful.

And to you—yes, you reading this. Thank you for buying this book. You didn't just purchase some pages and a matte cover—you took the first step in declaring war on apathy. You decided your life is worth showing up for, and I respect the hell out of that.

Now let's make sure you get the most of it. Download the free workbook that goes along with this book at www.escapingthedrift.com. You took the first step. Let's make sure you finish strong.

Be free. Level up. Live on purpose.

To get the most updated version of this workbook, or to connect with additional training information, please scan this QR code.

APPENDIX

ESCAPING THE DRIFT EXERCISES

I designed these twenty exercises to help you apply some of the lessons from *Escaping the Drift* to your own life. Each exercise is structured to deepen your understanding and drive actionable change. If you want it to work, YOU HAVE TO DO THE WORK! Go to www.escapingthedrift.com and download the free workbook that goes along with this book, featuring these exercises and dozens more.

EXERCISE #1: MINDSET SHIFT

Identifying Negative Mindsets:

- Reflect on a recent situation where you felt stuck or defeated. Describe it in detail.

  ____

  ____

  ____

- What thoughts or beliefs contributed to feeling this way?

____

____

____

Reframing Challenges:

- List three challenges you are currently facing.

____

____

____

- For each challenge, write down a positive reframe or a potential solution.

____

____

____

EXERCISE #2: EFFECTIVE COMMUNICATION

Crafting Requests:

- Think of a situation where you need to ask for help or negotiate something. Write down your request clearly and assertively.

____

____

____

For a full workbook, go to www.escapingthedrift.com

- Role-play this request with a friend or family member to practice your communication skills.

Writing Persuasive Emails:

- Choose a past situation where you needed to escalate an issue to a higher authority.

____

____

____

- Draft an email, including facts, figures, and respectful language.

____

____

____

____

____

EXERCISE #3: UNDERSTANDING THE RULES

Identify the Rules:

- Choose an area of your life (e.g., career, education, personal relationships) and list the written and unwritten rules you believe apply.

____

____

____

____

____

- How do these rules impact your decisions and actions?

___

___

___

Evaluating Your Approach:

- Reflect on a recent challenge you faced. How did you navigate the rules?

___

___

___

- Were there any unwritten rules you overlooked? How could recognizing them have changed the outcome?

___

___

___

EXERCISE #4: CREATIVE PROBLEM-SOLVING

Finding Loopholes:

- Think of a situation where you faced a strict rule. How could you creatively work within or around this rule to achieve your goal?

___

___

___

For a full workbook, go to www.escapingthedrift.com

- Write down at least two potential strategies.

___

___

___

Applying Creativity:

- Choose one of the strategies you identified and develop a detailed action plan to implement it.

___

___

___

___

___

- What resources or support will you need to execute this plan?

___

___

___

EXERCISE #5: EFFECTIVE COMMUNICATION AND NEGOTIATIONS

Crafting Persuasive Requests:

- Think of a request you need to make in your personal or professional life.

___

___

___

- Write down the key points and supporting arguments. Practice delivering this request confidently and assertively.

____

____

____

____

____

Negotiation Techniques:

- Reflect on a past negotiation where you were successful. What techniques did you use?

____

____

____

- Identify a current situation where you need to negotiate and apply these techniques.

____

____

____

EXERCISE #6: STRATEGIC NETWORKING

Building Relationships:

- Identify three people in your network who are skilled at finding and leveraging angles.

  ____

  ____

  ____

- Reach out to them and schedule a time to discuss their approaches and learn from their experiences.

Mastermind Groups:

- Research local or online mastermind groups that align with your interests and goals.

  ____

  ____

  ____

- Join at least one group and actively participate in discussions and activities.

EXERCISE #7: MANAGING RISK AND BETTING ON YOURSELF

Assessing Risk Aversion:

- Reflect on your comfort level with financial risk. Are you more inclined toward a steady salary or a commission-based role?

  ____

  ____

  ____

- Write down the pros and cons of each approach for your personal situation.

____

____

____

____

____

Setting Personal Goals:

- Set a personal or professional goal that requires betting on yourself. Create a detailed plan with milestones and timelines to achieve this goal.

____

____

____

____

____

- Identify potential challenges and strategies to overcome them.

____

____

____

____

____

EXERCISE #8: UTILIZING THE POWER OF "BECAUSE"

Incorporating "Because":

- Write three sales pitches for different scenarios, each incorporating the word "because" to explain the reason behind your request or suggestion.

____

____

____

____

____

- Practice delivering these pitches and observe the reactions.

____

____

____

Testing Compliance:

- Conduct a small experiment in your daily interactions where you use "because" to make requests. Track the responses and analyze the effectiveness.

____

____

____

- Reflect on how this technique impacts your communication and persuasion skills.

____

____

____

EXERCISE #9: OVERCOMING COMFORT ZONES

Comfort Zone Analysis:

- Reflect on a recent situation where you stayed within your comfort zone. What was the outcome?

____

____

____

- Identify areas in your life where you are hesitant to step outside your comfort zone.

____

____

____

Action Steps:

- List three actions you can take this week to push yourself out of your comfort zone.

____

____

____

- Commit to completing these actions and reflect on the experience.

___

___

___

EXERCISE #10: BUILDING ACCOUNTABILITY

Accountability Partner:

- Identify someone who can act as your accountability partner. Share your goals and plans with them.

___

___

___

- Schedule regular check-ins to discuss your progress and any challenges you face.

Public Commitment:

- Share one of your major goals publicly, either through social media or with a group of friends or colleagues.
- Use the public commitment to motivate yourself to stay on track.

EXERCISE #11: ADDRESSING LABELS AND EXCUSES

Challenging Labels:

- Identify any labels or excuses you use to justify negative behavior or lack of progress (e.g., "I'm always late," "I'm just a procrastinator").

  ____

  ____

  ____

- Write down counter-statements that challenge these labels and promote a growth mindset.

  ____

  ____

  ____

Positive Self-Talk:

- Practice positive self-talk by writing down affirmations that reinforce your ability to change and succeed.

  ____

  ____

  ____

- Read these affirmations daily, especially when you feel tempted to revert to old habits.

For a full workbook, go to www.escapingthedrift.com

EXERCISE #12: EMBRACING PERSONAL RESPONSIBILITY

Taking Ownership:

- Think of a recent situation where you relied on others instead of taking responsibility. Describe the situation and its outcome.

____

____

____

- How could taking personal responsibility have changed the outcome? What steps can you take to ensure you take ownership in the future?

____

____

____

Developing Independence:

- Identify a task or goal that you have been hesitant to tackle on your own.

____

____

____

- Write down the steps you need to take to complete it independently. Commit to taking the first step within the next week and document your progress.

____

____

____

____

____

EXERCISE #13: CONSUMING POSITIVE CONTENT

Content Audit:

- Keep a journal of the content you consume over the next three days (e.g., social media, news, books, music). Note how each piece of content makes you feel.
- Identify any negative content that brings you down and develop a plan to reduce or eliminate it from your daily routine.

____

____

____

____

____

Curating Positive Inputs:

- Make a list of books, podcasts, and other media that inspire and motivate you. Commit to incorporating these into your daily routine.

____

____

____

- Reflect on how consuming positive content affects your mood and productivity over time.

____

____

____

EXERCISE #14: PRACTICING MANTRAS

Creating Mantras:

- Write down a list of your limiting beliefs. For each belief, create a positive, empowering mantra that counters it.

____

____

____

____

____

- Practice reciting these mantras daily, especially during moments of self-doubt.

Visual Reinforcement:

- Place your mantras in visible locations (e.g., on your bathroom mirror, as your phone wallpaper).
- Regularly read and recite your mantras to reinforce positive thinking and self-belief.

EXERCISE #15: EMBRACING A POSITIVE MINDSET

Daily Positivity Practice:

- Start each day by listing three things you are grateful for and three positive affirmations about yourself.
- Reflect on how starting your day with positivity affects your overall mindset and interactions with others.

____

____

____

Spreading Positivity:

- Make it a habit to share positive feedback and encouragement with others in your circle.
- Observe how spreading positivity impacts your relationships and the overall atmosphere of your social and professional environments.

____

____

____

EXERCISE #16: EVALUATING YOUR CURRENT NETWORK

Network Audit:

- List all the people currently in your professional network. Identify their roles and how they contribute to your growth.

____

____

____

____

____

- Assess the diversity of your network. Are most people from the same industry or background? How might this impact your growth?

____

____

____

Identifying Gaps:

- Reflect on areas where your network is lacking. What types of professionals or skills are missing?

____

____

____

- Create a plan to connect with individuals who can fill these gaps.

___

___

___

EXERCISE #17: EXPANDING YOUR NETWORK

Meetup Exploration:

- Search for local meetups or networking events related to your industry or interests. Make a list of upcoming events you could attend.

___

___

___

- Choose at least one event to attend in the next month. Prepare an elevator pitch to introduce yourself effectively.

___

___

___

Cross-Industry Networking:

- Identify three industries outside your own where you could benefit from connections.

___

___

___

- Research events or groups within these industries and plan to attend or join at least one.

EXERCISE #18: BUILDING AUTHENTIC RELATIONSHIPS

Getting Personal:

- Practice asking deeper questions when meeting new people. Instead of "What do you do?" ask "Tell me about you."
- Record your experiences and note how these conversations impact your connections.

____

____

____

Consistency in Communication:

- Develop a system to regularly check in with your network (e.g., monthly emails, quarterly calls).

____

____

____

- Create a calendar reminder to follow up with new contacts made at events.

EXERCISE #19: PRACTICING HUMILITY

Humility in Action:

- Think of a recent success. How can you acknowledge others' contributions to this success?

  ____

  ____

  ____

- Write a note or email to someone who helped you, expressing your gratitude and acknowledging their role.

  ____

  ____

  ____

  ____

  ____

Learning from Mistakes:

- Reflect on a mistake you made recently. How did your ego play a part in it?

  ____

  ____

  ____

- Write down what you learned from the mistake and how you can approach similar situations differently in the future.

  ____

  ____

  ____

For a full workbook, go to www.escapingthedrift.com

EXERCISE #20: ENGAGING IN CONSTRUCTIVE FEEDBACK

Seeking Feedback:

- Identify a trusted colleague or friend and ask them for honest feedback about your behavior and how you handle your ego.

  ____

  ____

  ____

- Reflect on the feedback and create an action plan to address any areas of improvement.

  ____

  ____

  ____

Giving Constructive Feedback:

- Practice giving constructive feedback to someone in your network. Focus on being specific, respectful, and supportive.

  ____

  ____

  ____

- Reflect on how the feedback was received and how it improved your relationship.

  ____

  ____

  ____

For a full workbook, go to www.escapingthedrift.com

RESOURCES

Baumeister, Roy F., and John Tierney. *Willpower: Rediscovering the Greatest Human Strength*. New York: Penguin Press, 2011.

Clear, James. "Let Your Values Drive Your Choices." Accessed April 23, 2020. https://jamesclear.com/values-choices.

Covington, Martin. "Self-Worth Theory: Retrospection and Prospects," in *Handbook of Motivation at School*, edited by Kathryn R. Wentzel and David B. Miele, New York: Routledge, 2016.

Crum, Alia, and Thomas Crum. "Stress Can Be a Good Thing If You Know How to Use It." *Harvard Business Review*, September 3, 2015. https://hbr.org/2015/09/stress-can-be-a-good-thing-if-you-know-how-to-use-it.

Dweck, Carol S. *Mindset: The New Psychology of Success*. New York: Random House, 2006.

Gleeson, Brent. *TakingPoint: A Navy SEAL's 10 Fail-Safe Principles for Leading Through Change*. New York: Touchstone, 2018.

Goggins, David. *Can't Hurt Me: Master Your Mind and Defy the Odds*. Austin, Texas: Lioncrest Publishing, 2018.

Goldsmith, Marshall, with Mark Reiter. *What Got You Here Won't Get You There: How Successful People Become Even More Successful*. New York: Hyperion, 2007.

Grover, Tim S. *Relentless: From Good to Great to Unstoppable*. New York: Scribner, 2013.

Hill, Napoleon. *Think and Grow Rich*. Cleveland: The Ralston Society, 1937.

Hillenbrand, Laura. *Unbroken: A World War II Story of Survival, Resilience, and Redemption*. New York: Random House, 2010.

Honnold, Alex, with David Roberts. *Alone on the Wall*. New York: W. W. Norton, 2015.

Konnikova, Maria. "How People Learn to Become Resilient." *The New Yorker*, February 11, 2016. https://www.newyorker.com/science/maria-konnikova/the-secret-formula-for-resilience.

Langer, Ellen J., Arthur Blank, and Benzion Chanowitz. "The Mindlessness of Ostensibly Thoughtful Action: The Role of 'Placebic' Information in Interpersonal Interaction." *Journal of Personality and Social Psychology* 36, no. 6 (1978): 635–42.

Mangurian, Glenn E. "Realizing What You're Made Of." *Harvard Business Review*, March 2007. https://hbr.org/2007/03/realizing-what-youre-made-of.

Owen, Mark. *No Easy Day: The Firsthand Account of the Mission That Killed Osama Bin Laden*. New York: Dutton, 2012.

Ruiz, Don Miguel. *The Four Agreements: A Practical Guide to Personal Freedom*. San Rafael, California: Amber-Allen Publishing, 1997.

Sudeikis, Jason, et al. *Ted Lasso*. Warner Bros. Television Studios, 2020–present.

The Farmer's Parable. Adapted from the traditional Taoist tale, commonly referred to as "Maybe So, Maybe Not." Modern retelling set in 1940s Nebraska. Public domain story.